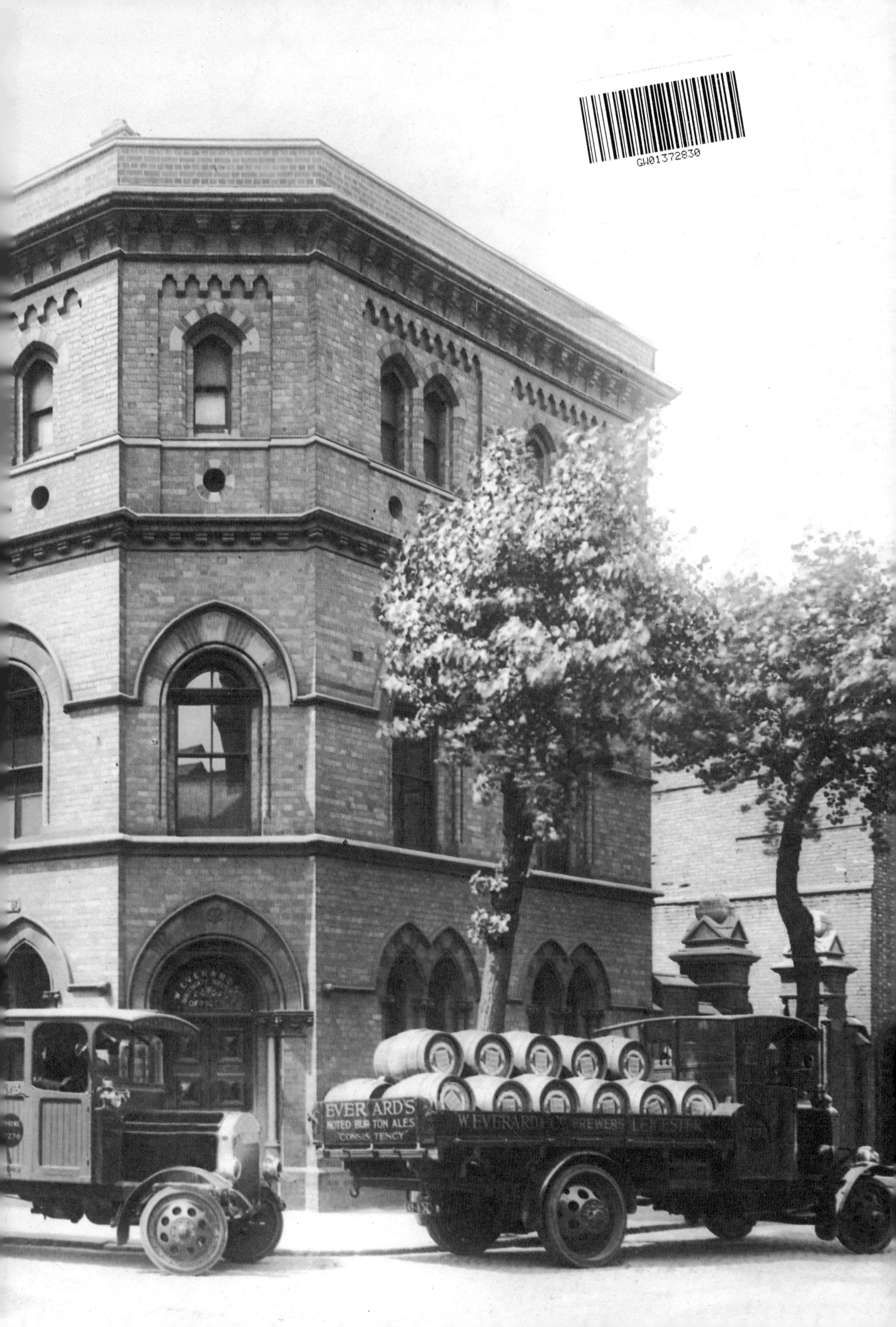
EVERARD'S
NOTED BURTON ALES
CONSISTENCY

EXCELLENCE through INDEPENDENCE

The First 150 Years of Everards Brewery
1849–1999

Excellence through Independence

Foreword

I feel extremely proud to be the custodian of our family business as it celebrates its 150th year.

Much has changed within our family, the brewery and the world at large, since 1849 when my great-great grandfather took the momentous decision to move from farming to brewing.

The passage of time means that much of this story is not known to those involved with us today. We therefore felt it appropriate to use this anniversary to capture and illustrate the history of our family business in a book which could then be shared with all interested parties.

People have always been at the heart of our business and its success. Their endeavours and support over five generations are represented within these pages and I see this book as a tribute to their loyalty, both past and present.

I take this opportunity to thank all those who have contributed their talent, time, artefacts and anecdotes towards the compilation of this book.

These are, of course, only the first few pages of our history and we now look forward, to the future and a new millennium, with a sense of optimism and excitement.

RICHARD EVERARD, D.L.
CHAIRMAN
May 1999

Contents

The Everard Family	5
The Everards of Thurlaston	6
William Everard, J.P. – the Founder	8
Southgate Street Brewery	12
Thomas William Everard, J.P., D.L.	16
Life at Bradgate House	18
W. Everard & Co.	21
The Burton Breweries	23
John Sarson & Son	26
Leicester and Burton	28
Sir William Lindsay Everard, J.P., D.L.	30
W. Everard & Co. Ltd	36
Everards Brewery Ltd	38
Patrick Anthony William Beresford Everard	40
'A Family Firm'	44
A Time of Change	46
The Everards Tiger	49
New Tastes for New Times	50
Castle Acres	52
Richard Anthony Spencer Everard, D.L.	56
A New Philosophy	59
Towards the Millennium	60
A Royal Beginning to the Next 150 Years	61
The Everards Estate	62
The Everards Company Philosophy	64

First published in Great Britain in 1999 by
Everards Brewery Ltd
Castle Acres
Narborough
Leicestershire
LE9 5BY

Acknowledgements:

Geoff Calderbank; Martin Capenhurst; John. H. Collier; Geoff Dye; Simon Everard;
Pick Everards; Dinah Henstock; William S. Hubbard; Gwynnyth & David Lawrence Jones;
John Lawrence Jones; Robert Lawrence Jones; The Leicester Mercury; Leicester Records Office;
Leicestershire Agricultural Society; Nat West Bank; Paula & Andy Oram; Thea Randall;
Bill Shooter; Staffordshire Records Office; Adrian Weston; Wigston Records Office.

Primary Research: Richard Everard

Research & Original Text: Christine Brooke & Fergus Sutherland

Editing & Additional Text: David Rae & Simon Ford

Picture Research & Design: Simon Ford

All rights reserved. No part of this publication may be reproduced, stored in a retrieval system, or transmitted in any form or by any means, electronic, mechanical, photocopying, recording or otherwise, without the prior permission of the copyright owner.

A CIP catalogue record for this book is available from the British Library.

ISBN 0 9535968 0 X

Printed and bound in Leicester, England by Taylor Bloxham Ltd.

Photography: Martin Capenhurst; The Leicester Mercury; The Everards Archive.

Page 23: View of Burton-upon-Trent by K. Thomas, 1840.
Reproduced by permission of the Trustees of the William Salt Library, Stafford.

Illustrations: David Barnett; Norman Shepherd

The Everard Family

The Everard Family Coat of Arms

The Everard family have been living in Leicestershire for many generations and can claim to be one of the oldest families in England. Their lineage stretches back before the Norman Conquest, in 1066, to the Saxon peoples who settled here centuries before.

The name 'Everard' is ancient, 'ever' meaning a wild boar, once a common sight in the English countryside. This species has always been a great hunting prize with its ferocity and tenacity becoming part of English legend, and is a symbol of steadfastness and courage.

From early times the Everard family was to be found living throughout a large part of England, settling in Berkshire, Bedfordshire, Staffordshire, Cambridgeshire, Kent, Northamptonshire, Suffolk and Leicestershire.

1507
Death of Roger Wygston, three times Mayor of Leicester.

1529
Death of William Everard of Shenton.

1536
Death of William Wygston, nephew of Roger, the richest citizen ever in Leicester.

1547
Death of King Henry VIII.

1556
Death of Richard Everard of Shenton.

1588
Death of John Everard of Thurlaston.

1588
Leicester is granted its Charter of Incorporation by Queen Elizabeth I.

1637
Death of Thomas Everard of Thurlaston.

1645
Royalist forces attack and capture Leicester during the Civil War.

1649
Execution of King Charles I.

1660
The monarchy is restored under King Charles II.

1685
Death of Joseph Everard of Thurlaston, son of John.

1689
Death of John Everard of Thurlaston, son of Thomas.

The Everards of Thurlaston

Above: A view of Leicester in 1775.

Right: Thomas Everard of Groby. (1781-1861)

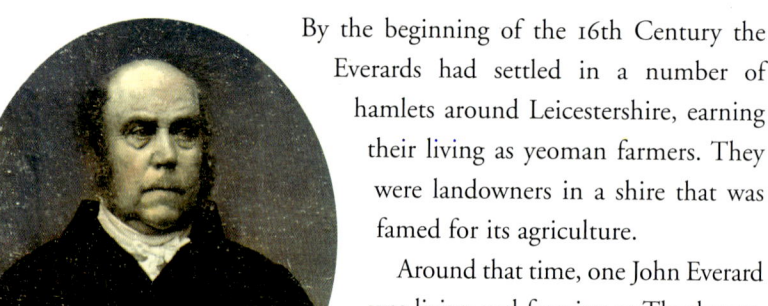

'At the age of twenty-nine, William Everard was to enter the new world of commerce and enterprise…'

The Stamford Arms, Groby.
William Everard's former home was to become an Everards pub in 1921.

By the beginning of the 16th Century the Everards had settled in a number of hamlets around Leicestershire, earning their living as yeoman farmers. They were landowners in a shire that was famed for its agriculture.

Around that time, one John Everard was living and farming at Thurlaston. He had three sons and three daughters, and when he died in 1588 he left his estate to his eldest son Thomas.

Thomas continued to farm and he also owned some land in Leicester Forest. He had two sons and six daughters and, when he died in 1637, an inventory of the household showed that his family were living a comfortable life. His goods and farm stock were valued at the respectable sum of £326.12s.8d, including £1.10s.0d in his purse and £27.10s.0d in his coffer. The house had seven rooms including the hall, the parlour and the little parlour (both used as bedrooms), a chamber over the parlour, a chamber over the house, a kitchen and a buttery. Furnishings included one table with chairs and stools, five bedsteads with mattresses and pillows, but no baths, washstands, jugs, basins or towels for washing! Knives and spoons would have been rarities and forks had only just arrived in England.

The Everard family continued to farm their land at Thurlaston for another four generations. It was Thomas's great-great-grandson Richard who, after marrying in 1738, moved to Groby as a yeoman tenant farmer of the Earl of Stamford and Warrington. His eldest son, Richard, was succeeded by his eldest son, Thomas, who married Mary Breedon of Ruddington on 5th August 1813.

Thomas and Mary's three daughters and six sons were born into a world in the throes of the Industrial Revolution. Three sons became merchants – Thomas in China, Richard in England, and John in Australia, where he was elected as a member of the Legislative Assembly of Victoria. Their eldest son, Breedon, became a farmer before forming a partnership with James and Joseph Ellis as Ellis & Everard, now a long established Leicester company, who celebrated their own 150th anniversary in 1998. At that time, the Everard family already had an interest in pubs as it is known that one Thomas Everard owned the Elephant and Castle at Thurlaston from 1818 to 1860.

Thomas and Mary's third son, William, recognised the opportunities being created by the rapidly growing industrial economy in Victorian Leicester. At the age of 29, he was to enter the new world of commerce and enterprise when he went into partnership to lease the brewery on Southgate Street in Leicester.

Groby Pool, Leicestershire. Groby was home to the Everard family for many years and the house above once belonged to Lindsay Everard's sister, Phyllis Logan.

Breedon Everard of Groby, later of Bardon (1814-82). Founder of Ellis and Everard, a long established Leicester company.

Leicester in the 1800s showing the increasing industrialisation.

1708
Birth of Richard Everard of Thurlaston, son of George.

1709
Death of George Everard of Thurlaston, son of Joseph.

1726
The first turnpike road to Leicester is opened.

1738
Marriage of Richard Everard of Thurlaston to Ann Denwell.

1738
Richard and Ann move to Groby.

1744
Birth of Richard Everard of Groby, son of Richard Everard of Thurlaston.

1753
The Leicester Journal, the town's first newspaper, begins printing.

1778
Marriage of Richard Everard of Groby to Mary Fletcher of Groby.

1781
Birth of Thomas Everard, son of Richard Everard of Groby.

1784
Death of Richard Everard of Groby.

1785
Work on Leicester's famous New Walk begins.

1796
John Sarson & Son, Wine Merchants, founded in Hotel Street, Leicester.

1805
Battle of Trafalgar.

William Everard, J.P. – the Founder

William Everard was born on 13th July 1821. He was born in a country where the Industrial Revolution was still in its infancy, and farming remained the largest single occupation. Even in Britain, where industrialisation was most advanced, there were many more domestic staff than factory workers, more blacksmiths than miners, and twice as many agricultural labourers as the total of all the workers in the entire textile industry. Throughout the country, large factories were a rarity and the old hand crafts still flourished.

Although increasing daily, in 1821 the population of Britain was still only 21 million – more than twice the figure for the United States. It would be another four years before the world's first passenger train ran between Stockton and Darlington, and a decade before Charles Darwin's voyage on *HMS Beagle* was to revolutionise mankind's conception of history.

William Everard had been born into a country that stood on the brink of transformation from the old to the new, one which was to take him from the agricultural world the previous generations of Everards had lived in, into the modern world of urban industry.

The Founder.
William Everard (1821-1892).

Above: Bow Bridge, Leicester.
The Industrial Revolution swept away most of old Leicester's medieval, half-timbered buildings.

Right: The Mitre and Keys Inn, early 1800s.
One of the oldest inns in Leicester, the Mitre and Keys was an Everards pub from 1931 to 1959. Sited on Applegate Street, it was demolished to make way for the Leicester ring road in the 1960s. Local legend tells of a tunnel which ran beneath it from St Nicholas's Church to the Castle.

William Everard married Mary Ann Billson on 27th March 1847. They had three children – John Billson who died aged four, Sophia Louisa who married Arthur Turle at the relatively late age of 32, and Thomas William who was to continue his father's work at the brewery.

William and his wife were running the farm at Narborough Wood House when, in common with many other landowners and farmers at the time, he saw the new opportunities offered by industry. On the 5th October 1849, in the eleventh year of the reign of Queen Victoria, he entered into partnership with Thomas Hull, a local maltster, taking over the brewery of Messrs Wilmot and Co. and leasing the brewery premises in Southgate Street from a William Bates.

It was a decision that carried a significant financial risk. William's hard work and his astute decision to buy into the brewing trade at a time of industrial and population expansion combined to make the business a rapid success.

Narborough Wood House, 1854.
This painting by F. Clarke shows Thomas and Louisa, the Founder's children.

'William Everard had been born into a country that stood on the brink of transformation from the old to the new...'

The Old Blue Boar Inn, c.1826.
An Everards pub from 1895 to 1972. It was here that Richard III stayed the night before the Battle of Bosworth Field in 1485. He brought his own massive oak four-poster bed which remained at the inn after he was defeated and killed. However, many years later, while the landlady was making the old oak bed, she discovered it had a false bottom where Richard had hidden £300. In 1613 the landlady was murdered by a maid who was looking for the treasure. The maid and her lover were both caught and hanged.

1812
A canal link between Leicester and London is established.

1813
Marriage of Thomas Everard to Mary Breedon of Ruddington.

1814
Birth of Breedon Everard, eldest son of Thomas Everard.

1815
Battle of Waterloo marks the end of Napoleonic Wars.

1819
Birth of the future Queen Victoria.

1821
Birth of the Founder, William Everard, son of Thomas Everard of Groby.

1821
Coronation of George IV.

1821
Death of Napoleon Bonaparte.

1825
Opening of the first railway line to carry passengers-the Stockton to Darlington line.

1828
The Duke of Wellington becomes Prime Minister.

1830
The first railway in Leicester opens.

1830
Coronation of William IV.

1831
Charles Darwin sets sail on *HMS Beagle*.

9

Excellence through Independence

Some of the first pubs acquired by William Everard included the King William IV (above) in Earl Shilton, The Old Swan (left) in Newbold Verdon and The Bull's Head Inn (bottom left) in Cosby.

The brewery became well established during William's forty-two years in charge. During this period there was a shift in status from the traditional, land-owning, political power brokers to the new industrialists. A new class of entrepreneurs, made wealthy through their efforts in brewing, even had a new name coined to describe them – the 'beerocracy'.

As a successful and responsible Victorian citizen, William took public service seriously and devoted a large amount of time to several public bodies. He joined the Leicester Highways Board on its constitution, and served for twenty years as its chairman.

He was an energetic supporter of the Conservative Party, arranging meetings, chairing political gatherings and entertaining candidates and speakers at his house, eventually becoming chairman of the Harborough Division.

Continuing to operate his farm as well as run his business, William also became prominent in local agricultural affairs as a member of the Chamber of Agriculture and the Leicestershire Agricultural Society, founded in 1833. Followed later by his son and then his grandson he was an enthusiastic participant and regularly showed his prize Shire mares and foals in competition.

When William died peacefully in his sleep at the age of 71 he was mentioned in his obituary as being 'of a kindly disposition, considerate and ever anxious to avoid offence.' He had been a successful farmer, brewer, public and family man and his legacy was to form a sound foundation for the Everards Brewery business of the future.

His personal achievements are reflected by the fact that at the time of his death, the company owned not only the Southgate Street Brewery but also an estate which totalled over forty pubs in and around Leicester.

William Everard's will, 1893.

'No effort should be found wanting in the production and supply of genuine ale of first-rate quality.' – William Everard

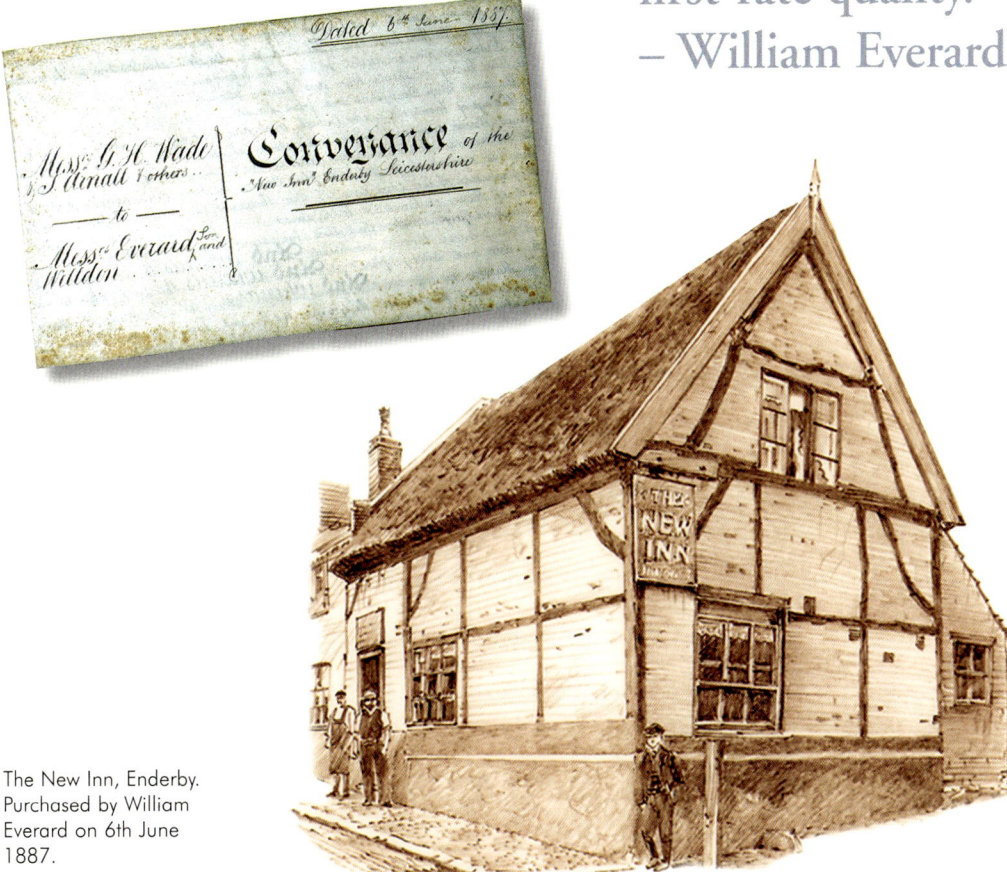

The New Inn, Enderby. Purchased by William Everard on 6th June 1887.

1832
Britain occupies the Falkland Islands.

1833
Abolition of slavery in the British Empire.

1837
Death of William IV.

1838
Coronation of Queen Victoria.

1841
Thomas Cook organises his first tourist excursion to a Temperance meeting in Loughborough.

1847
Marriage of the Founder, William Everard to Mary Ann Billson.

1849
William Everard establishes a partnership with Thomas Hull, a local maltster, and they acquire Messrs Wilmot & Co's brewery on 5th October.

1851
Birth of Thomas William Everard, son of the Founder, William Everard.

1851
First horse-drawn double decker bus introduced.

1853
Vaccination against smallpox made compulsory in Britain.

1855
Livingstone discovers the Victoria Falls.

1855
First iron Cunard steamer crosses the Atlantic (nine and a half days).

Southgate Street Brewery

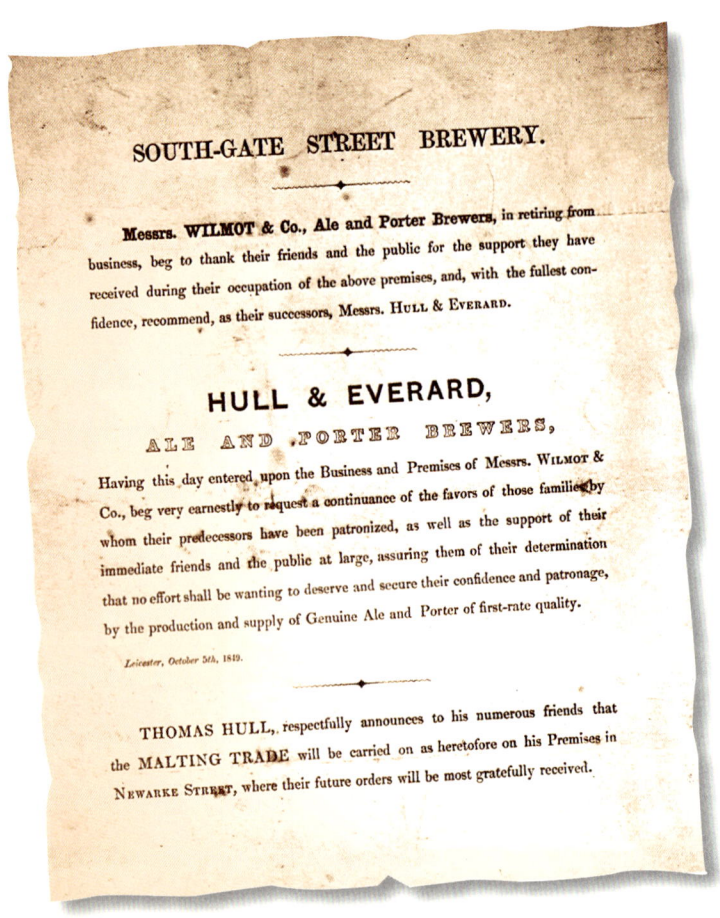

By the middle of the 19th Century the Industrial Revolution was in full swing, and Britain was evolving at a rate never seen before nor since. Large factories were springing up and the new canals and railways were able to move people and goods around the country more efficiently than ever before. The small market towns were exploding with workers flooding in from the countryside. Leicester was no exception as first the hosiery and then the footwear industries rapidly transformed it into a modern industrial city.

This new industrial population needed places to live in, things to do and places to eat and drink. The old local beerhouse brewers could not service this new mass of people, and so entrepreneurs, realising the opportunities that existed, began buying breweries and building new ones.

William Everard was the initiator and the driving force behind the new brewery enterprise. Thomas Hull continued in his business as a maltster, but did not feature very actively in the affairs of the partnership. From the very first days the brewery was run by a member of the Everard family.

The brewing operation they acquired on Southgate Street was quite typical of breweries at the time. The leases stipulated that the terms were 'a clear yearly rent of £100 of lawful money of Great Britain by four equal quarterly instalments,' for which they would acquire 'all the plant, copper vats, casks and other implements now in the said brewery.'

The relatively large scale of the business is shown by some of the items from the inventory. There were 'two coppers (and) two vats of one thousand gallons each,' allowing them to produce around fifty barrels of beer at any one time. There were also 'one hundred and thirty six dozen quart stone bottles (and) one hundred and thirty seven dozen pint bottles,' possibly to hold the beer that they sold to the local farms, especially during the harvest.

Everard – a new name in brewing.
The original announcement from 5th October 1849.

The population in Leicester grew rapidly during the Industrial Revolution.

'The Everards of Thurlaston, a family of farmers for generations, had become brewers.'

A plan of the proposed new Southgate Street Brewery.

Horsefair Street, Leicester, 1870.
In the 19th Century, the heart of old Leicester was transformed as new houses, shops and factories progressively replaced the medieval buildings.

1857
British financial crisis after speculation in USA railroad shares.

1860
Abraham Lincoln elected 16th President of the USA.

1861
Death of Thomas Everard, father of the Founder.

1861
Death of Prince Albert the Prince Consort.

1864
Louis Pasteur invents pasteurization.

1866
Aeronautical Society of Great Britain founded.

1866
'Black Friday' on London stock exchange.

1867
Game of badminton devised.

1870
Education Act makes primary education compulsory.

1872
Licensing Act enacted for the first time in Britain.

1873
Modern game of lawn tennis introduced.

Excellence through Independence

The brewing business of Messrs Everard and Hull thrived by providing for the needs of Leicester's expanding industrial population.

It was a good time to be a brewer in Britain, and the second half of the 19th Century saw a huge expansion in output across the country. Brewing science and technology made great strides, and the use of steam engines helped brewers to mechanise their processes. Breweries began to grow in size and complexity and industrial brewing became both a major employer and also a prominent contributor to the country's economy.

In the 1870s it became obvious that the old brewery in Southgate Street could no longer cope with the demand, and William decided it was time to build a new one. He commissioned his nephew John Everard, a partner in the local architect's practice of Pick Everard, to design a purpose-built, state-of-the-art tower brewery. The new Southgate Street Brewery began full production in 1875 and is described in the article to the right, taken from 'Modern Leicester' in 1901.

Messrs Everard, Son and Welldon, Brewers, Southgate Street

Among the leading brewers of Leicestershire Messrs Everard, Son and Welldon, Brewers, Southgate Street, Leicester, occupy a high position. The business has been established 50 years, and since its commencement has continued in popular favour throughout the district. The brewery is what is technically known as a 30-quarter plant brewery, and is a handsome red-brick building of imposing elevation, centrally situated at the corner of Southgate and Castle Streets: it is equipped with mash tuns, coppers, coolers and refrigerators, these being of the best and most modern character, while the fermenting vessels are provided with temperators, parachutes, and every appliance to facilitate the work and ensure its being performed in a steady and reliable manner. Storage rooms are provided for malt and hops, and a stock of the best English hops is always kept in reserve. Attached to the brewery are large vats and cellars for the storage of beer, while adjoining is a large yard for washing and purifying the casks previous to filling them. The water used for brewing purposes is perfectly pure and one of the best brewing waters to be found in Leicestershire; it is procured from artesian wells sunk on the premises, some 300ft. deep. The proportion of malt and hops is adjusted with a nicety so as to provide a uniform character in the beverage, with the result that Messrs Everard, Son and Welldon's beers and stouts are always of the same good quality, and we should say it is extremely rare for a cask to be returned on their hands. The 'India Pale Ale,' of a bright amber colour, particularly pleasing to the palate, and tasting well of the hop; and the famed 'Diamond Ale,' a full-flavoured nutritious beverage, are specialities of the firm; their Stout is also well spoken of by the medical profession for its purity and its nourishing qualities. Brewing is now a science, and no greater proof of the success of this brewery could be adduced than that, notwithstanding the extraordinary competition in the trade during recent years, Messrs Everard, Son and Welldon have been able, not only to hold their own, but to make large advances, and, by offering a superior beer to the public at a moderate price, to practically meet all opposition.

Above:
The keystone from Southgate Street Brewery.

Right:
The new Everards Brewery on Southgate Street was a bold statement of confidence in the business at that time. It was fitted with the most modern brewing equipment available and designed not just for the present, but for the future too.

The growing production capability of the brewery was matched by a steady growth in the number of pubs owned by the company. Between 1862 and the start of the new century, Everards had acquired the freeholds or leases of over 70 pubs. These were mainly in Leicester but also extended a presence into villages right round the city.

Clockwise from top:

The Antelope Hotel, Silver Street, Leicester. Dating from 1666, the Antelope Hotel in Silver Street was an Everards pub from 1888 to 1978. Like many old Leicester buildings it eventually made way for modern development.

The Blue Boar, Southgate Street, Leicester.

The Railway Inn (now the Soar Bridge Inn), Barrow-on-Soar.

The Bulls Head, Leicester Forest West.

The Railway Inn, Ratby.

The Old Horse, London Road, Leicester.

1876
Alexander Graham Bell invents the telephone.

1877
Queen Victoria declared Empress of India.

1878
Edison invents the phonograph.

1878
Edison and Swan produce the electric light bulb.

1884
The Leicestershire Football Club divides to form the Leicester Fosse (later Leicester City) soccer team and a rugby side which retains the name Leicester Football Club ('the Tigers').

1886
Benz builds the first motor car.

1888
Thomas William Everard marries Florence Muriel Nickisson from London.

1890
Charles Leeds Welldon joins the partnership which becomes Everard, Son and Welldon.

1891
Birth of Lindsay Everard, son of Thomas Everard.

1892
Death of the Founder, William Everard.

1892
Everard, Son & Welldon lease the Bridge Brewery, Umplett Green Island, Burton-upon-Trent (est. 1865), from Henry Boddington & Co Ltd.

1893
Zip fastener invented in USA.

15

Thomas William Everard, J.P., D.L.

Left: The Second Generation. Thomas Everard (1851-1925).

Right: Thomas's wife Muriel with their children William Lindsay and Phyllis Muriel.

Above: Leicestershire Agricultural Society Catalogues, 1929 and 1888, showing the Everards sponsored Challenge Cup.

Thomas Everard was appointed High Sheriff of Leicestershire in 1905.

Thomas William Everard was born on the 8th of September 1851, the year the Great Exhibition was staged by Prince Albert in the Crystal Palace in London. He was the youngest of Mary and William's three children. John, his elder brother, died at the age of four and his sister Sophia Louise was born only eighteen months before him. Having babies was fraught with risks in Victorian times and Thomas's young mother, Mary, died within a year of his birth. His thirty year old father never remarried.

Thomas joined his father's firm at an early age and quickly became very involved in his work at the brewery. He was so fond of his work he did not like to take holidays.

In 1890 a new partnership was formed to run the company – Everard, Son and Welldon. The partners were Thomas, his 69-year old father William, and a local wine and spirits merchant, Charles Leeds William Welldon. William died on the 28th of December 1892, and Thomas took over the running of the brewery.

Thomas and Muriel Everard (centre) at the opening of the Groby cattle trough in 1909. The Victorians and Edwardians realised that a regular supply of good, fresh drinking water was crucial to the health of both man and beast, and carried out many projects with the result that the death rate from disease fell dramatically.

Thomas Everard married Florence Muriel Nickisson of London on the 28th of September 1888. She was twenty-five and he was thirty-seven. They had two children – William Lindsay, born in 1891, and his sister Phyllis Muriel, born three years later.

Thomas enjoyed both country and urban life and was an active member of the Leicestershire Agricultural Society, as were both his father and his uncle Breedon before him.

He continued the Everards tradition of public service and, like his father, he became a J.P. before being made a Deputy Lieutenant of the County, and, in 1905, High Sheriff.

Thomas was a keen public benefactor and in 1923 he presented two plots of land to the city. The Corporation named them 'Everard Place' (now under St Nicholas Circle) and they were dedicated as open land for the use of the people of Leicester. In 1915 he donated the altar, reredos, oak panels and communion rails to his local church at Newtown Linford.

Muriel was also an active figure in the local community. In 1909 she opened the new Groby Cattle trough (it was inscribed with the words, 'A Merciful Man is Merciful to His Beast'), and during World War I she spent time helping injured soldiers during their convalescence.

In the years of war between 1914 and 1918, millions of lives were lost and many servicemen were injured. The 'Home Front' was to become as important as the battle zones, both for supplying the soldiers in action, and for tending to the casualties when they returned home.

Muriel Everard hosted parties for convalescing soldiers at Bradgate House during the 1st World War.

17

Life at Bradgate House

As the company prospered, Thomas moved his family from the farm at Narborough Wood House, first to Stoneygate in Leicester, and then to Nanpantan Hall in Charnwood Forest. Finally he leased the imposing Bradgate House, the Leicestershire seat of the Earls of Stamford and Warrington, who coincidentally had been his grandfather's and great-grandfather's landlords at Groby.

Bradgate House, like all the great Edwardian houses, required a lot of staff. The indoor household was led by the housekeeper, Miss Bennet, who ran a strict regime. She lived in the house and had the extra responsibility of caring for the family's pet parrot, 'Polly', in her own room. Mr Baum, the butler, remained in the Everard family service until he died. The cook was assisted by the kitchen maid and the scullery maid, the head housemaid by the second and third housemaids. There were also at least three parlour maids and two footmen.

Bradgate House.
Sold after the death of Thomas Everard in 1925, it was demolished not long afterwards.

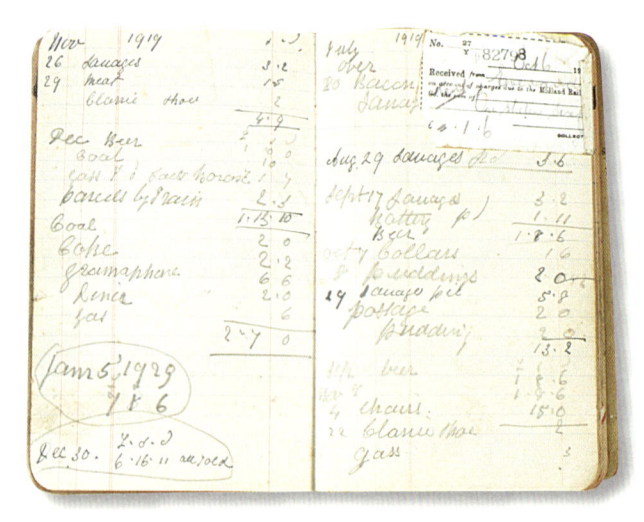

William Henstock's grocery book for December 1919 records the purchase of a gramophone for Bradgate House for the sum of six guineas.

'Polly', the family's parrot.

A family gathering in the grounds of Bradgate House.

The outdoor household was led by William Henstock, the head coachman and groom, who was in charge of the stable boys, three grooms and a cowman. He also looked after the herd of Jersey cows. The children would often dress them up for carnivals and family celebrations and ride on their backs as well as enjoying the supply of fresh milk they provided for the household.

Thomas Everard kept the highest standards both at the brewery and at Bradgate House and he always insisted that the stable yard had to be immaculate, with 'not a matchstick to be found.'

Henstock used to drive Thomas to the brewery every day in a pony and trap, and even after the family bought a car he still travelled to the brewery in this manner at least once a week. Henstock also had the responsibility for the daily shopping for the house. This ranged from the regular purchases of the usual groceries to unusual items like a gramophone which was bought for six guineas in December 1919. He ordered coal, bought lotion for the horses, delivered parcels to the London train and paid the chimney sweep and the scissor grinder.

Although horse-drawn transport was still in regular use, cars were becoming more prevalent.

Thomas and Muriel Everard are pictured here in an early chauffeur driven car with the registration AY 322.

'Thomas Everard kept the highest standards both at the brewery and at Bradgate House.'

Drivers and Coachmen at Lindsay Everard's 21st Birthday Party in 1912. The different styles of dress indicate that whilst most have arrived by horse and carriage, several have come by car. William Henstock is seated in the middle row, second from the right.

1894
Birth of Phyllis Muriel Everard, daughter of Thomas Everard.

1895
Marconi invents the wireless telegraph and radio in Italy.

1897
Queen Victoria celebrates her Golden Jubilee.

1898
Everard Son & Welldon lease the Trent Brewery, Burton-upon-Trent.

1899
W. Everard & Co. is formed.

1899
Bill Hubbard Snr. joins the company.

1900
First trial flight of the Zeppelin.

1901
Death of Queen Victoria. Edward VII becomes king.

1901
End of the 'Century of Steam' and beginning of the 'Century of Electricity'.

1901
W. Everard & Co. purchase the freehold of the Trent Brewery.

1903
The Wright brothers successfully fly a powered aeroplane.

1903
20 mph speed limit for motor cars introduced.

1905
Thomas Everard appointed High Sheriff of Leicestershire.

Excellence through Independence

Muriel Everard on a shoot.
As well as a social activity, these shoots played an important role in the household economy at Bradgate by providing food for the staff and the family.

The Everards entertained regularly and were well-known in local society. They were members of the Quorn Hunt and, although Thomas disliked being away from his work, they did holiday occasionally in Scotland where they enjoyed stalking and fishing. Muriel Everard was a keen sportswoman and a good shot, although it was quite unusual for a woman to take part in such activities in those days.

Bradgate House was a hive of activity, and what with daily living, house and garden parties, school treats and the sartorial demands of Thomas's various offices, the household generated a lot of laundry. William Henstock's wife, a trained laundress, was employed full-time solely to do this. It was a job which started on the Monday and finished on the Saturday. She had no machines to help her, and a lot of the fabrics demanded special care and attention. Wilson's and Sunlight soap were applied by scrubbing brush. Sheets were boiled in coppers, then starched. Everything was rinsed and mangled and hung in the special drying ground, then folded, mangled and left again for a whole day. The rest of her week was spent ironing the clean clothes, a job that could sometimes take all night.

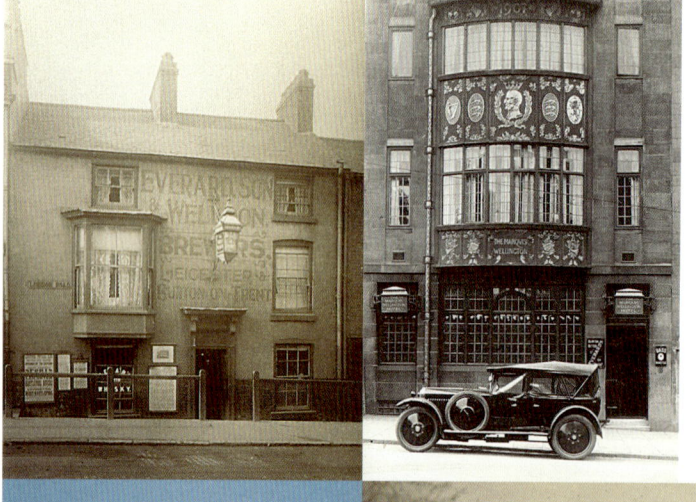

The Marquis Wellington, London Road.
An Everards pub since 1893, the Marquis Wellington was built on the site of a turnpike and its distinctive façade was created in 1907.

20

W. Everard & Co.

In 1890's England, Everard, Son & Welldon were operating in a country dominated by the Industrial Revolution. Although there was now a concentrated urban market to service, the pub trade was being challenged by the Temperance Movement (which was very active in Leicester), competition from sports like association football, and the arrival of a new craze, music hall, which, ironically, had begun as an entertainment in pubs. By the end of the Victorian era, however, British breweries were producing over forty million barrels of beer per annum.

On the 19th October 1899, fourteen days after the 50th anniversary of the founding of the company, the partnership of Everard, Son & Welldon was dissolved and W. Everard & Co. was formed in its place. Charles Welldon received £21,000 for his share, and the company became the sole property of the Everard family.

1899 also saw the arrival of Bill Hubbard Snr. beginning a family connection that was to continue through his son for over seventy-five years. He was initially employed as a clerk, but soon became Thomas Everard's right-hand man. He had his own office beside Thomas in the heart of the Southgate Street building from where he could oversee the office staff and the brewery operations.

Above: Deeds showing the transfer of pub ownership to T.W. Everard.

Left: The Barley Mow, Granby Street, Leicester. Bought in 1904, the Barley Mow was once accessible by tram, as this picture shows.

'The company became the sole property of the Everard family.'

Bill Hubbard Snr. worked for Everards for 55 years, through two world wars and the reigns of six monarchs.

The Blue Bell, Desford. A long established pub which joined the Everards Estate in 1901.

1909
Henry Ford introduces his Model T family car and sells nearly 16 million.

1909
Manufacture of bakelite heralds the beginning of the 'plastic age'.

1910
Death of Edward VII. George V becomes king.

1912
S.S. Titanic sinks on her maiden voyage.

1913
De Montfort Hall in Leicester opens for the first time.

1914
Assassination of Archduke Ferdinand starts World War I.

1915
Tank with caterpillar tracks invented in England.

1917
Marriage of Lindsay Everard to Cornelia Ione Kathleen Armstrong from Moyaliffe Castle, Co Tipperary in St. Peters Church, Eaton Square, London on the 28th of September 1917.

Excellence through Independence

Ancient Gravestone Revealed At A Leicester Hotel

A CENTURIES-OLD gravestone, which has been the subject of much comment for years through being fixed in the wall of what is perhaps the oldest fireplace in Leicester, has been fully revealed to view.

The gravestone, which was in the tap room of the Globe Hotel, Silver-street, Leicester, was in the wall of the old-fashioned bake oven chimney.

Workmen who are rebuilding the chimney removed the gravestone, which still bears the Christian names of young people who, apparently, were all members of the same family.

Many of the letters are obliterated, but the names of Thomas, who died at the age of eleven, Katherine, aged four, who died on March 1, 1693, and Elizabeth can be clearly seen. It is believed they were all members of a family of Cooke.

WELL 160 FEET DEEP

In the cellar of the Globe is a 160 feet deep well of clear spring water, and from it was drawn water when the house, many years ago, brewed its own beer.

The grandson of one of the old freeholders, Mr. Tom Jarvis, scratched his name and date, January 29, 1880, on one of the panes of glass in the smokeroom windows with a diamond, and the cutting can be seen there now.

In years gone by the Globe was a market house, and was used at the hiring fairs by the farmers and landed proprietors to engage their farm servants for the year.

The Globe, Leicester, at the corner of Carts Lane and Silver Street, and pictured here in 1861, is a pub steeped in history. In 1938, workmen renovating the pub discovered that the fireplace in the snug contained an ancient gravestone with an inscription bearing the name of Thomas Alfred Cooke, aged 11, who died at the start of the 15th Century. In the cellar they found a well of clear spring water dating from the days when the pub brewed its own ale. Many years later, several rare old beer mats were discovered in the roof space.

The Tudor Hotel, Tudor Road, Leicester. A new pub for a new century.

The 20th Century began with a period of economic downturn, and some breweries closed or were forced to amalgamate to survive. Although the expansion in the Everards estate of the 1880s and 1890s had slowed down, pubs were still being acquired, and in 1901 the company built and opened a brand new establishment, the Tudor Hotel.

The outbreak of war in 1914 brought conscription and many of the company staff left to join up. Breweries also had to deal with the effects of the introduction of the Defence of the Realm Act which limited opening hours for licenced premises, rationed raw materials and ordered the dilution of beer.

The post-war depression years saw even more brewery closures and amalgamations, but, throughout these troubled times, Thomas and Bill Hubbard Snr. ensured the brewery made sufficient returns. They continued to purchase pubs, adding more to the estate between 1922 and 1925 than in the whole of the 1930s and 1940s combined. In 1921 they also acquired the Stamford Arms in Groby, where Thomas's grandfather had lived. In the year 1920-21, the brewery produced over 55,000 barrels of beer, an output that was not to be matched for many decades as recession and war took their toll on the economy of the country.

In the final years of his life, Thomas became too ill to visit the brewery, and Bill Hubbard Snr. would visit him at Bradgate House to discuss company business. On the 1st of January 1925, Thomas Everard, the second generation of Everards to run the company, passed away peacefully in his sleep at the age of 73.

The Burton Breweries

Burton-upon-Trent has long been famous as a town which produces great beer. The Burton water was perfect for brewing the bitter, thirst-quenching 'pale ales' which captured the nation's taste-buds in the 1800s. These pale ales became so popular that by the 1890s the town of Burton was producing a tenth of all Britain's beer output.

At the end of the 19th Century Everard, Son & Welldon was one of five prominent breweries in Leicester. The others were the All Saints Brewery Co, Leicester Brewing & Malting Co, H.H. Parry, Welch Bros and Hoskins. Burton had almost thirty!

Increasing competition encouraged brewers to develop other outlets for trade, and so many of them began to buy public houses which would then sell only their beer. By the 1890s the expanding pub estate, the need for more beer production and the fame of pale ales, led Everards inexorably to Burton.

As a result, in 1892 Everard, Son & Welldon leased the Bridge Brewery, Umplett Green Island, from Henry Boddington & Co Ltd. The Bridge Brewery had a capacity of over 10,000 barrels of beer per year, but demand for Everards Burton Ale grew so strong that an even bigger operation was soon needed.

The Burton Bridge Brewery.
The brewery was the first Burton home of Everards and stood on an island in the middle of the River Trent.

'By the 1890s the expanding pub estate, the need for more beer production and the fame of pale ales, led Everards to Burton.'

View of Burton-upon-Trent by K. Thomas, 1840.

1917
Lindsay Everard serves in France with the 1st Life Guards during WWI until 1919.

1918
Armistice signed between Allies and Germany.

1919
Birth of Bettyne Ione Everard, daughter of Lindsay Everard.

1919
Lady Astor becomes the first woman MP.

1919
Alcock and Brown make the first non-stop flight across Atlantic.

1920
W. Everard & Co. acquire John Sarson & Son Ltd.

1920
Marconi open first public broadcasting station.

1922
BBC founded.

1922
Birth of Patrick Anthony William Beresford Everard, son of Lindsay Everard.

Excellence through Independence

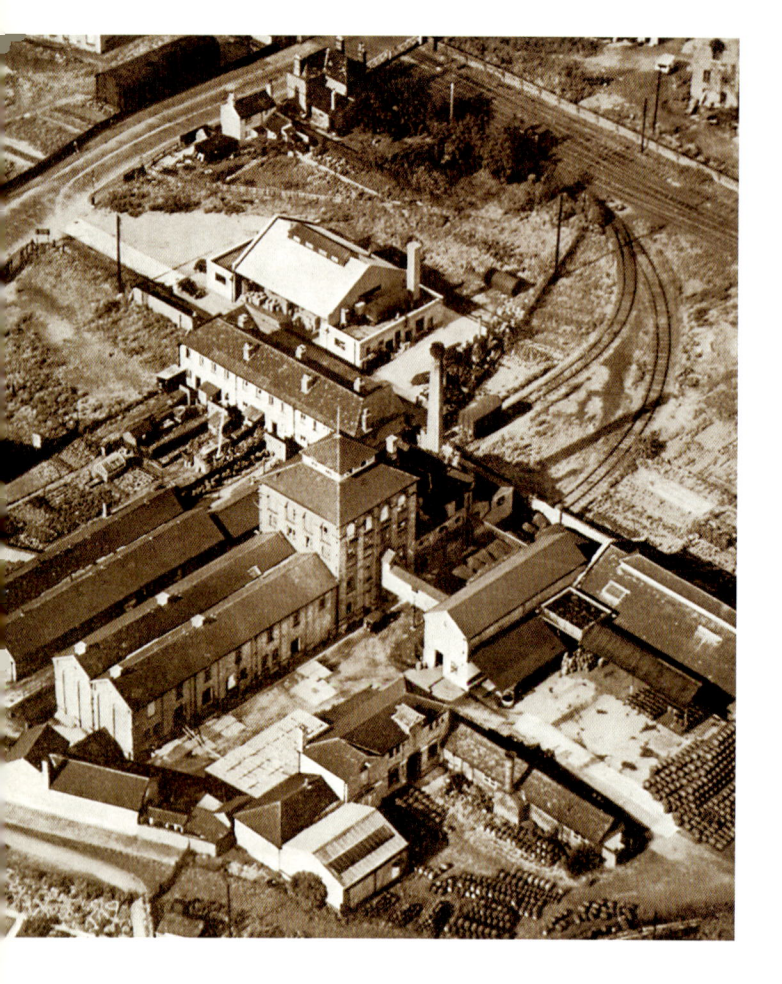

The Trent Brewery had been built in 1881 by Thomas Sykes, a Liverpool brewer. In 1885 he signed a new 99-year lease for the property from the Marquess of Anglesey at £49 per annum for 'the plot of land situated between Walker's Brewery and the Dale Street railway crossing, including the brewery, storerooms, stabling and cottages.' However in 1896, the Trent Brewery Co. went into voluntary liquidation.

On 17th February 1898 W. Everard & Co. leased the Trent Brewery and ceased operating the Bridge Brewery that June. The new operation was so successful that, on 18th January 1901, Thomas Everard bought the freehold for £9,000. It was later to be renamed the Tiger Brewery.

Most of Everards public houses were in Leicestershire, and the beer produced in Burton had to be transported to the Southgate Brewery for distribution. Burton was built upon a complex network of railway lines, and all the breweries used trains to deliver raw materials and transport their beer. As well as the brewery, Everards also owned a maltings at Wood Street on the Bond End Branch and regularly used the line to Leicester until the 1920s.

A rare aerial view of the Trent Brewery showing the locomotive tracks which linked the site to the unique Burton railway system.

The Trent Brewery.
The stack in the foreground vented the smoke from the coal-fired boilers which produced the steam to drive the brewery plant.

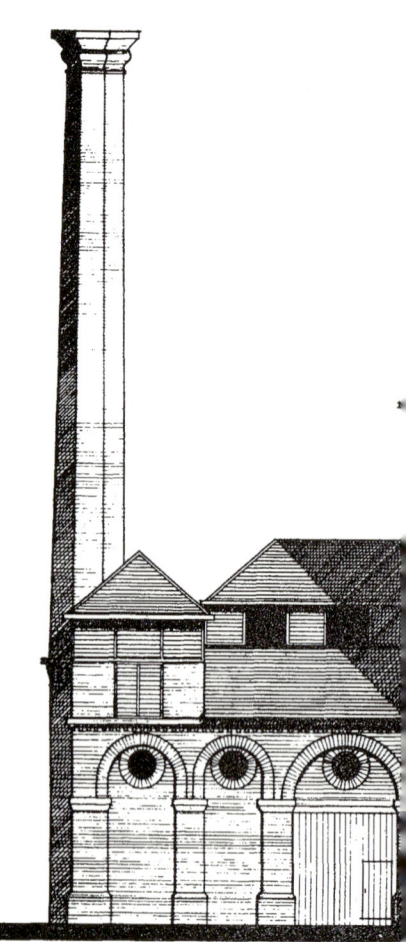

The Albion Vaults, Burton.
Although a brewer in Burton for almost a century, the Albion Vaults was the only pub which Everards ever owned there.

For many years Everards had no pubs in Burton, primarily because they had all been bought up by the other breweries before they arrived there in 1892. Their only chance came in 1935 when the last free house in Burton, the Albion Vaults, came up for auction. Everards wanted to purchase the pub, but, not wishing to advertise the fact to avoid a bidding war, they decided to use a Mr Chaplain to do the bidding for them. His instructions were to up the bid every time Bill Hubbard, sitting apparently disinterested in the proceedings, rubbed his nose. The subterfuge was successful and Everards acquired their only outlet in Burton for £10,300. The changing fortunes of Burton-upon-Trent meant that the pub was eventually sold in 1962.

ALBION VAULTS SOLD FOR £10,300.

Messrs. Everard's the Purchasers.

THE LAST FREE HOUSE.

Unusual interest centred in the sale this afternoon of the Albion Vaults, 32, High Street, the well-known licensed premises which have the distinction of being the only "free" house in Burton. The premises were offered at auction at the Queens' Hotel by Messrs. John German and Son. The property is freehold and fully licensed. Included in the sale are the licensed premises, dwelling house accommodation, the offices known at "Imperial Chambers," and the outbuildings occupying an area of 661 square yards, with a frontage to High Street of 26 feet.

The property belongs to Burton Feoffees and has come into the market through the falling in of the lease. The licensee is Mr. Norman Cartmell, to whom it was recently transferred from Mr. E. H. Clarke, for whom Mr. Cartmell managed it for many years.

The Albion Vaults was sold this afternoon for £10,300.

The purchasers were Messrs. W. Everard and Co., of Leicester.

Bidding started at £6,000 and rose rapidly to £10,100. The chief bidders were Mr. A. J. Flint (of Messrs. Flint, Marsden and Bishop, solicitors, Derby), and a representative of Everard's. At £10,100 there was a long pause. Then the bidding resumed by £100 bids and the Everard representative made the winning bid of £10,300—£100 in advance of the pre-ultimate bid.

UNIQUE SALE.

There was not a very large company of potential buyers. Among those present was Sir Herbert Evershed, J.P.

Mr. Guy German, the auctioneer, described the sale as unique in the history of Burton. It had never happened before, he said, and might never happen again, that anyone should offer for sale the last remaining free house in the world headquarters of brewing.

John Sarson & Son

An 1898 price list featuring an illustration of the façade of the original shop in Hotel Street.

Part of the central vault at Millstone Lane.

John Sarson & Son Ltd, Horsefair Street, 1952 with the company's Austin vans outside.

As the 20th Century progressed, competition between pubs encouraged a steady expansion in the range of products on offer. During their first seventy years in business, Everards had become not only a supplier of beer to pubs, but pub owners themselves. In 1920 they took this growth a significant step forward with the purchase of the wine and spirit merchants John Sarson & Son. This acquisition allowed them not only to supply all the requirements for beer, wine and spirits to their own pubs, but also to gain an increased foothold in the expanding free-trade market.

Founded in 1796 by John Sarson, the company was based in Hotel Street, Leicester, and operated as a high quality store supplying groceries and alcoholic beverages, in a similar manner to London's famous Fortnum & Mason. They specialised in fine wines, ports and sherries, and their catalogues read like the index from a book of famous vineyards. John Sarson & Son were not only a supplier to the licenced trade, however, and many famous private houses were stocked from their cellars. The wine and spirit side of the business became so successful that the grocery division was closed in the 1890s.

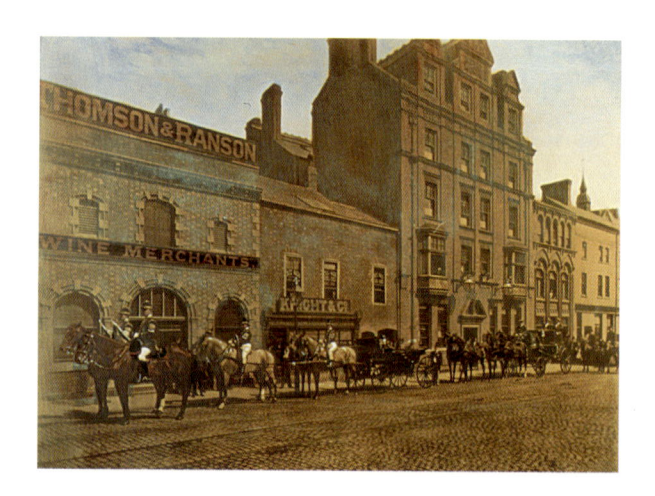

Horsefair Street in 1895 showing the Thomson and Ranson Ltd premises at number 15.

In 1875 Colonel John Edward Sarson had become the third generation of his family to run the company. He had been Managing Director for almost forty-five years when Thomas Everard purchased the business from him in 1920.

In 1923 Everards acquired Thomson and Ranson Ltd, wine and spirit merchants, and John Sarson & Son moved into their premises at 15 Horsefair Street. The old cellars in Hotel Street continued to be used until 1928 when the stock was moved to new premises in Millstone Lane, finally severing a connection that stretched back to the reign of King George III.

The first branch-shop of the new and expanding wine and spirits department was opened in Narborough Road in 1927. The off-licence division became a very successful part of the company's business and at its peak operated from almost sixty premises, selling not only wines and spirits but also significant quantities of draught beer for home consumption.

The painting of John Sarson which now hangs in the Everards board room.

In addition to their range of fine wines, John Sarson & Son Ltd were also renowned for top quality cigars, and their speciality teas and coffees, as shown by these price lists from the Great War.

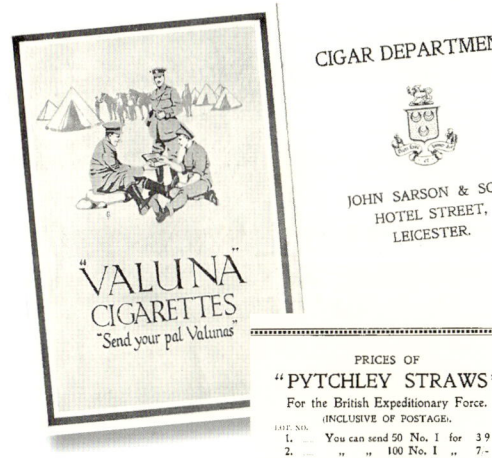

1922
Lindsay Everard and his family move into Ratcliffe Hall.

1923
W. Everard & Co. acquire the old established firm of Thomson & Ranson Ltd, in Horsefair Street and John Sarson & Son Ltd move into their premises.

1923
Arthur Willis appointed Head Brewer.

1924
Lindsay Everard appointed Deputy Lieutenant for Leicestershire.

1924
Lindsay Everard appointed High Sheriff of Leicestershire.

1924
Lindsay Everard elected the MP for Melton constituency.

1924
Everards begin using steam-powered drays.

1924
Frozen food invented by Birds Eye in United States.

1925
Death of Thomas Everard, son of the Founder.

1925
W. Everard & Co. Ltd registered as a limited liability company.

1925
The Charleston is the dance of the day.

1926
General Strike in support of the coal miners.

Leicester and Burton

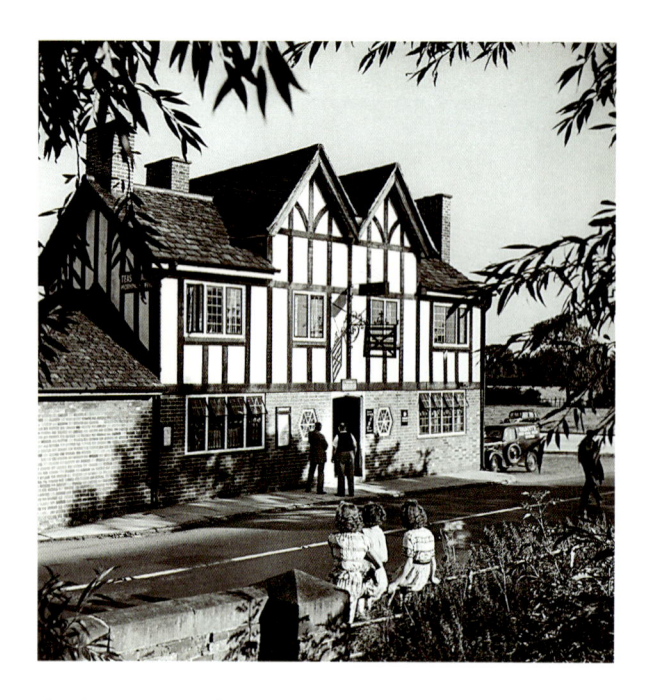

The Gate Hangs Well, Syston. Purchased in 1924, it features an unusual pub sign which bears part of the following poem:
*This gate hangs well
And hinders none,
Refresh and pay
And travel on,
Turn in at the gate
And taste of the tap,
Drink and be merry
And keep off the strap.*

The Age of Steam.
Although horse-drawn drays were used to deliver beer locally, Everards became well-known for their steam-powered lorries, which regularly travelled the road between Leicester and Burton.

By the early 1920s Everards had moved almost completely away from railway transport. In 1923, the last year they used trains, only 109 barrels of beer were sent by rail.

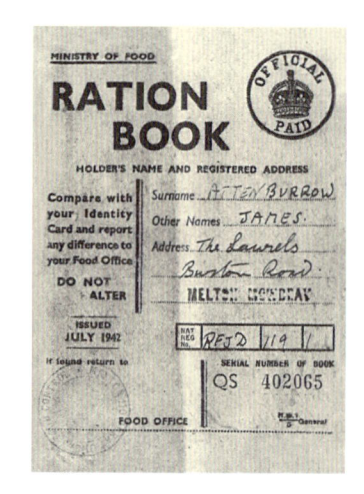

From 1924 the brewery moved all their goods and products between Burton and Leicester using steam-powered drays. A 1924 inventory lists two 6-ton and one 10-ton Super Sentinel articulated, 6-wheel steam lorries, and two 5-ton Foden steam wagons as well as five petrol lorries and three horse drays.

The steam wagons were reliable and economic to operate, and Everards continued to use them until June 1946, when they were finally replaced by petrol lorries. Wartime rationing of vital supplies, like petrol, meant that both the steam wagons and the horses had to be pressed into service again as the only economic form of transport available. The Sentinels and Fodens are still fondly remembered in Burton, except by the local fire brigade which was occasionally called out to quench the fires started by the sparks flying from their chimneys!

There were also distinct hazards in using the horse-drawn carts in the ice-covered cobbled yards during the winter months. The only way into the brewery yard for the draymen was to walk the horses and drays at a good speed down the slope before swinging the cart around at the last minute, hoping that they ended up in the correct place at the loading bay!

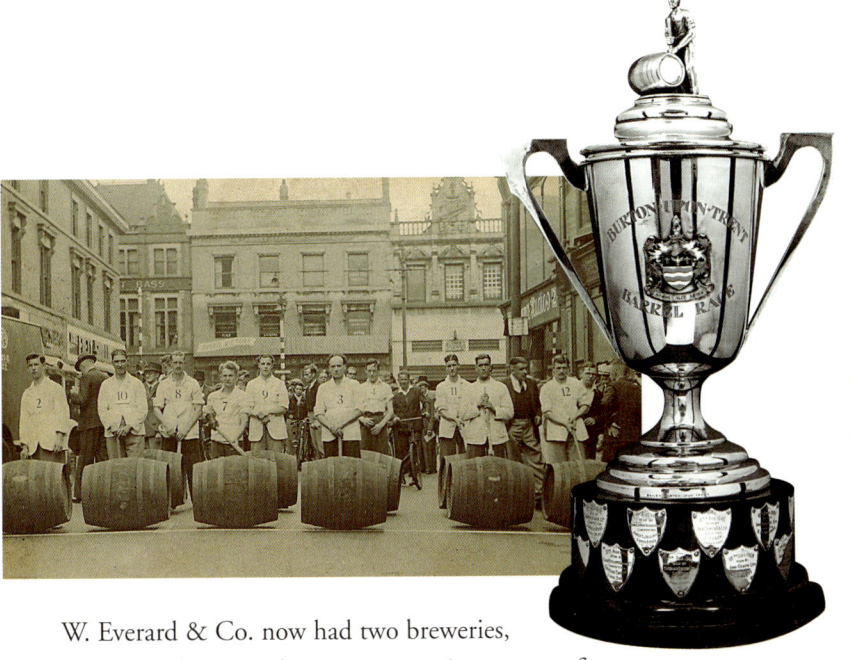

The Burton Barrel Rolling Competition. A unique annual event held in the streets of the town, involving coopers and draymen from all the Burton Breweries.

W. Everard & Co. now had two breweries, a wine and spirits division, a growing estate of freehold pubs and many free trade customers. Their main local competitor was the Leicester Brewing & Malting Co Ltd. Operating out of the Eagle Brewery in Upper Charnwood St from 1890, they owned fifty licenced houses, a maltings, and, in 1920, they took over the Welch Brothers' St Martins Brewery in Loseby Lane and their tied estate.

Competition was keen, and eventually a meeting was called between the two companies. The two managers, Bill Hubbard Snr. for Everards and a Mr Turner for the Leicester Brewing Company, arrived at a unique solution, agreeing to divide Leicester into two areas and not to compete on the other's territory. For how long this arrangement operated is not recorded, but in 1952 the Leicester Brewing & Malting Company was acquired by Ansells of Birmingham who closed the brewery and took over their estate of licenced houses.

The Victory, Aylestone Road, Leicester. An Everards pub since 1902, the Victory was originally called the Bedford Hotel. It was renamed when Leicester Tigers won the John Player Cup in 1980 for the third successive year.

Everards dray fleet always kept pace with developments in the world of transport, adopting the latest types of vehicle.

1927
John Sarson & Son open their first branch shop on Narborough Road, Leicester.

1928
John Sarson & Son Ltd vacate the old cellars in Hotel Street and move to Millstone Lane.

1928
All women over the age of 21 get the vote.

1930
Harry Jarratt, who later becomes a director, joins Everards.

1930
Amy Johnson makes her record-breaking flight to Australia and later in the year opens Ratcliffe Aerodrome.

1930
Frank Whittle begins design of turbo-fan jet engine.

1931
Bill Hubbard Jnr. joins Everards.

1931
Production of beer ceases at the Southgate Street Brewery, Leicester.

1932
Lindsay Everard tours North Africa and Europe in his Puss Moth.

1933
Hitler comes to power.

1933
Everards establishes a Managed House Department.

1936
W. Everard and Co. becomes Everards Brewery Ltd.

Sir William Lindsay Everard, J.P., D.L.

William Lindsay Everard was 34 years old when his father died and control of the company passed to him. He had been educated at Harrow School and then Trinity College, Cambridge. During World War I he served in the Leicestershire Yeomanry from 1914 to 1917, rising to be adjutant. He saw active service in France with the 1st Life Guards until the end of the hostilities in 1919.

On the 28th of September 1917, during the war, he married Cornelia Ione Kathleen Armstrong from Moyaliffe Castle, Co. Tipperary in St. Peters Church, Eaton Square, London. They had two children, Bettyne Ione in 1919 and Patrick Anthony William Beresford in 1922, the year that they moved into Ratcliffe Hall.

After the war, Sir Lindsay followed the family tradition and was active in local public life. He became a J.P. in 1923, Deputy Lieutenant of the County in 1924 and High Sheriff in 1924. He also sponsored the construction of several new village halls in his constituency.

The Third Generation.
Sir William Lindsay Everard (1891-1949).

The marriage of Sir Lindsay and Ione Armstrong took place while he was on leave from active service.

Following in his father's footsteps.
Sir Lindsay became both High Sheriff and Deputy Lieutenant for the County of Leicestershire.

Lady Ione, Bettyne, Tony and Sir Lindsay with his Puss Moth aeroplane 'The Leicestershire Fox' in the hangar at Ratcliffe.

With Sir Lindsay's grandfather's long service in local government, it was perhaps not such a large step for him to look to national politics and to Westminster. In 1924 he stood as the Conservative Party candidate for the Melton constituency in the infamous 'Zinoviev Letter' General Election which brought down the first ever Labour government. Using Ratcliffe Hall as his headquarters, he campaigned using the slogan, 'If you work hard for Everard, he'll work hard for you.' Stanley Baldwin's Conservatives won with an overall majority of more than 200 seats, one of whom was Melton's new Member of Parliament, Lindsay Everard.

He took his seat in Westminster for the first time in November 1924 and served his constituency for over twenty years. In 1939 he received a knighthood from King George VI for his services to commerce and aviation. Bad health eventually forced him to retire from Parliament in 1945 at the relatively young age of 54.

A telegram from former Prime Minister Stanley Baldwin congratulates Lindsay Everard on his 1929 election victory.

A Christmas card from Ione Everard.

'If you work hard for Everard, he'll work hard for you.'

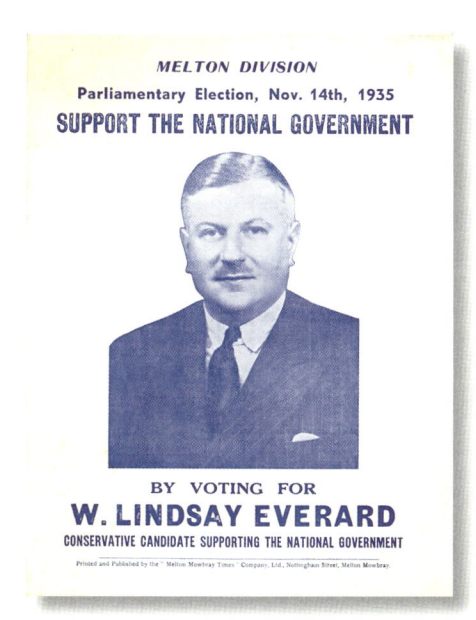

Sir Lindsay's election poster for his successful campaign in the 1935 General Election, the third time in a row that he had won the Melton Division.

Ratcliffe Hall – home of the Everard family.

1936
Death of King George V. Edward VIII becomes king and later abdicates to be succeeded by George VI.

1936
The Everards Brewery Men's Darts League is set up.

1936
Bill Hubbard Jnr. appointed an Everards director.

1937
Supermarket trolleys invented in USA.

1938
Lindsay Everard, MP for Melton, tables questions in Parliament highlighting Nazi Germany's military build-up.

1938
Neville Chamberlain signs agreement with Hitler at Munich.

1938
A new bottling and soft drinks hall is built at Southgate Street.

1938
Lindsay Everard appointed honorary Air Commodore to 605 (County of Warwick) Squadron Royal Auxiliary Air Force.

1938
Ballpoint pen invented by Lajos Biro.

1939
Lindsay Everard awarded a knighthood.

1939
Ratcliffe Aerodrome becomes the base for 6 Ferry Pool.

1939
Radar used as early warning system.

Excellence through Independence

Sir Lindsay had a lifelong interest in aviation, gaining his private pilot's licence in the 1920s. He became president of the Royal Aero Club, the County Flying Club, and the Leicester Aero Club. The latter, with over 900 members, was the biggest flying club in Britain in the early 1930s. He also supported them by donating several aircraft.

He was a practical man and had the useful idea of painting place names onto the top of gasometers to help pilots navigate. (These were painted over at the outbreak of World War II!).

On the 6th September 1930 he opened his own private aerodrome in fields near Ratcliffe Hall. The inauguration ceremony was attended by over five thousand people and one hundred light aircraft. The guest of honour was the aviator Amy Johnson who had achieved world-wide fame by flying solo to Australia only three months before. A flight of Siskins performed a stunt fly-past – in formation and tied together! During the 1930s the airfield held regular air shows and competitions, including annual meetings of the Fédération Aéronautique Internationale.

The opening of Ratcliffe Aerodrome, in 1930, was a major event and was attended by Amy Johnson, the famous aviator.

Sir Lindsay often used Parliamentary recesses to undertake airtours in Europe and the Near East. His was one of three planes which visited Cairo, Alexandria, Damascus, Constantinople, Athens, Venice, Cannes and Paris in 1932.

Air races were extremely popular in the 1930s. They were great social events, and during one race in 1932 the house party at Ratcliffe flew in five aeroplanes to Skegness and had a picnic and a dip in the sea, before flying back to the house in time for dinner!

M.P. AIR RACE VICTOR
900-MILE FLIGHT OVER DESERT

CAIRO, Tuesday.

British entrants did well in the International Air Rally here. The "Oases Circuit" contest, the most severe of the three tests, being over 900 miles of desert, from oasis to oasis, was won by Mr. W. Lindsay Everard, M.P.

He also gained the "Oases Cup." Squadron-Leader F. O. Soden took third prize in the "Oases Circuit." Mr. Everard's 'plane was a Dragon Moth, while Squadron-Leader Soden piloted his own Gypsy Moth.

Another British entrant, Mr. Guy Robson, won the fastest speed prize in a miniature Schneider Cup race over a 230-mile course. Mlle. Loutfia, an Egyptian woman, arrived first, but was disqualified. — Reuter.

THE MEMBER FOR MELTON

Mr. Lindsay Everard, who has been Conservative M.P. for the Melton Division of Leicestershire since 1924, is one of the best-informed men in the House of Commons on the subject of aviation. He possesses one of the finest private aerodromes. It adjoins his Leicestershire home at Ratcliffe Hall.

Mr. Lindsay Everard and Miss Spooner.

M.P.'s Air Tour Of Near East Ends

MR. LINDSAY EVERARD DUE BACK AT DESFORD TO-MORROW

WEATHER permitting, Mr. W. Lindsay Everard, M.P. for the Melton Division, who has been on an extensive air tour in the Near East, will arrive back at Desford aerodrome to-morrow afternoon. He is due at Heston about lunch time, and expects to reach Desford by 3.30.

The party has consisted of three 'planes—Mr. Everard's Puss Moth, piloted by Miss Winifred Spooner; another Puss Moth, belonging to Mr. W. D. McPherson, last year's squash rackets champion, who took with him as passenger Mr. J. W. Fox, son of the former M.P. for Tamworth, and a third machine piloted by Mr. W. R. D. Perkins, M.P. for Stroud.

Mr. Sidney Brown, joint hon. secretary of the Leicestershire Aero Club, has received a number of postcards from Mr. Lindsay Everard during the last few days giving an account of the last stages of the tour.

The fliers gave a flying party at Cairo a fortnight ago, and took up about 20 people who had never been aloft before. They then flew to Alexandria, and circled over H.M.S. Glorious, the aircraft-carrier.

The following day they left Cairo, and Friday saw them at Amman, having flown via Gaza and Maan. They spent Friday night at Damascus, and thence to Aleppo, Constantinople, and Athens.

Before reaching Athens they flew over Gallipoli, and saw where the famous landings were made.

They have since flown by way of Sophia, Zagreb, Venice and Cannes to Paris, whence they will leave on the final "hop" to-morrow.

An article from the Leicester Mercury, 15.10.32. In the 1930s, the flying MP's adventures attracted regular interest from the media.

1939
Britain and France declare war on Germany.

1939
Igor Sikorsky constructs the first helicopter.

1940
On the night of 19th November Leicester is blitzed by German bombers and 108 people are killed.

1940
Development of penicillin as an antibiotic.

1941
Tony Everard commissioned as a lieutenant with the Royal Horse Guards.

1941
Japanese attack on Pearl Harbor brings USA into World War II.

1942
Soft drinks production at Southgate Street is controlled under a wartime scheme.

1942
FIDO – device for clearing fog from airfields invented.

1944
Tony Everard wounded in action in France.

1944
Automatic calculator invented in USA.

1945
Sir Lindsay Everard retires as MP for Melton.

1945
First atomic bomb detonated in New Mexico.

Excellence through Independence

Sir Lindsay Everard (second from the right) was an acquaintance of King Edward VIII and was often seen in his company.

'Sir Lindsay's 1930's airtours also took him into Adolf Hitler's Germany.'

Sir Lindsay's Hornet Moth.

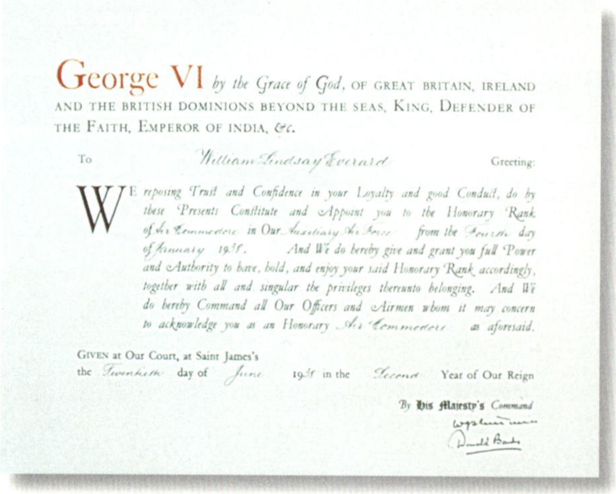

In recognition of his services to aviation Sir Lindsay was appointed an Honorary Air Commodore.

Sir Lindsay's 1930's airtours also took him into Adolf Hitler's Germany. The Treaty of Versailles at the end of World War I had laid down precise limits for the German armed forces, including strict controls on its air force. However, Melton's MP observed that Hitler's government was circumventing these restrictions. On his return he presented questions in the House of Commons which revealed the disturbing fact that, while in Britain there were 1,000 amateur flying club members, Germany had 50,000.

Along with other aviation-minded MPs he persuaded Neville Chamberlain's government to take action. As a result the Auxiliary Air Force was given increased resources, and the Civil Air Guard and the Air Defence Cadet Corps were formed, the Leicester squadron being the first. Sir Lindsay donated aircraft to each, helped to launch the Air Training Corps and instigated the scheme to provide flying training, at five shillings an hour, through his chairmanship of the Leicester County Flying Club.

In 1938 he was appointed Honorary Air Commodore to the 605 (County of Warwick) Squadron Royal Auxiliary Air Force which later took part in the Battle of Britain. He was also appointed one of the first four Commissioners of the Civil Air Guard.

The Leicester Blitz.
The victims of World War II included over 100 people who died during the bombing suffered by Leicester on the night of 19th November 1940.

When war was declared on the 1st of September 1939 all private flying was banned. Sir Lindsay handed over his private airfield at Ratcliffe to the war effort, and, due to its proximity to the Midlands aircraft factories, it became the base for 6 Ferry Pool of the Air Transport Auxiliary. The pilots and ground staff were billeted in Ratcliffe Hall for the duration of the war where they and the family were looked after by two footmen and George Smart, the family butler.

The pilots at Ratcliffe had to fly their way to and from the factories through the Midlands smog, the black-out and the barrage balloons. Access to the aerodrome buildings was across the grass runway, and visitors and pilots knew that they had to be ever vigilant to avoid being struck by incoming aircraft!

The heavy industry in the Midlands made it an obvious target for air raids, and although Leicester was officially designated as a 'safe area', this did not prevent German bombers blitzing the city on the night of 19th November 1940. It was the first time that the city had been directly involved in warfare since the Civil War, and over a hundred people were killed.

Town Hall Square, Leicester 1942.
Rally for the war effort with John Sarson & Son premises just visible in the background.

1945
'Black markets' in evidence for food, clothing and cigarettes

1945
14th August – Japan surrenders to USA and Allies, end of World War II.

1945
Microwave oven invented in USA.

1946
Everards retire the steam wagons and replace them with lorries.

1946
Harry Jarratt rejoins the company after war service.

1947
Tony Everard resigns his Commission and joins the family company on 14th October.

1947
Bill Lofthouse joins the brewery – forms the Everards Sports and Social Club and the Everards Ladies' Darts League.

35

W. Everard & Co. Ltd

When Sir Lindsay took over the company in 1925 the new limited company was renamed W. Everard & Co. Ltd. With his commitments as a working MP taking up much of his time, the responsibility for the day-to-day management of the company fell to Bill Hubbard Snr..

The inter-war years were marked by further rationalisation and amalgamation in the brewing industry. During the Depression, in the early 1930s, unemployment in Britain rose to over three million and industry suffered. W. Everard & Co. Ltd, strong as it was, did not escape the economic downturn unscathed and it faced a crisis in 1931 that required radical action.

The government, searching for new sources of revenue, increased taxation on beer by a penny a pint. Nationally sales tumbled. Everards output fell by almost a fifth and took five years to recover. Consequently the decision was made to close the brewing operation at Southgate Street, which was under threat from the proposed new Leicester inner ring-road. Instead the site became the company's distribution centre, and all brewing was transferred to Burton-upon-Trent.

From top: Some of the pubs which joined the estate between the wars.
- The Braunstone, Narborough Road, Leicester. Opened in 1925, it attracted customers who travelled out of the city on many different forms of transport!
- The Cradock Arms, Knighton, Leicester.
- The Lancaster Arms, Desford.
- The Bradgate, Newtown Linford.
- The Blackbird (Interior & Exterior), Blackbird Road, Leicester. A new pub built by Everards which opened shortly before war was declared in 1939.

36

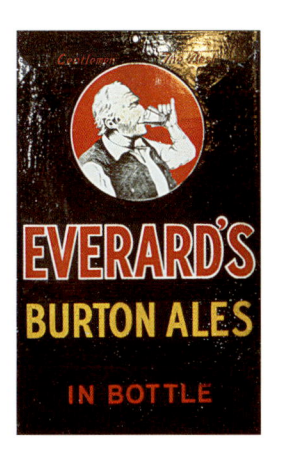

Despite the Depression, the 1930s were still a time of progress for Everards. Harry Jarratt joined as a clerk in 1930 but within three years he was helping Bill Hubbard Snr. to restructure the company by setting up a new Managed House Department. Pub acquisition continued and included the Dog and Gun at Keyham and the Blackbird in Leicester, the latter built by Everards and opened in 1939 just before the outbreak of World War II.

At the Trent Brewery, Head Brewer Arthur Willis was producing a Best Mild, a Bitter and a Best Bitter (brand names for beers did not become common until after the war). The brewery's biggest seller at that time was mild, a favourite with industrial workers looking for a refreshing ale to quench their thirsts.

Nationally the shift away from darker, heavier beers to lighter, brighter ales and even lagers was gaining momentum. Some breweries were even experimenting with beer in cans. Many brewers also began to look seriously at advertising as a means of marketing their products. This, however, was curtailed by the war when widespread rationing meant that all the beer that could be produced was easily sold.

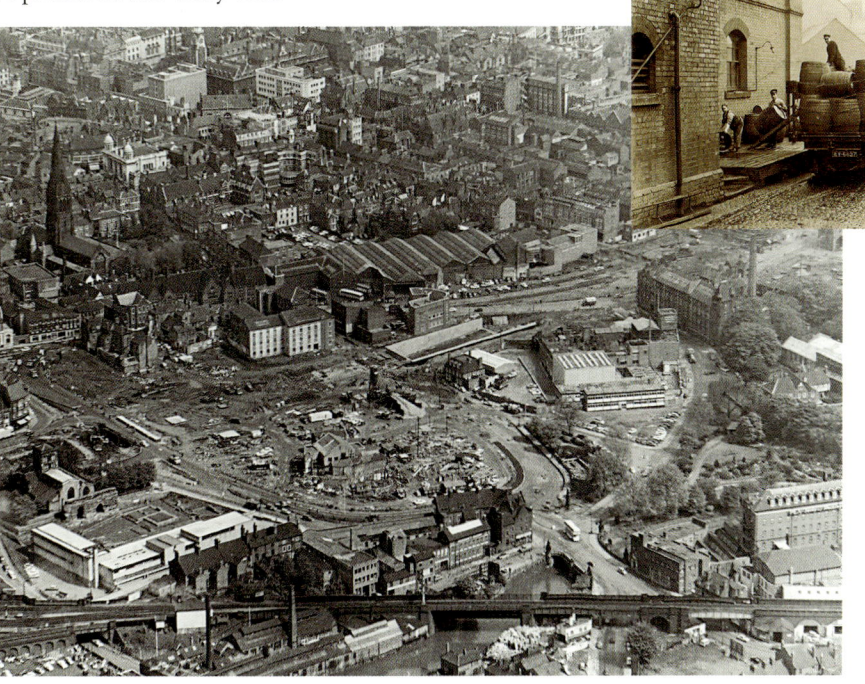

Head Brewer Arthur Willis inspects the quality of another Everards brew.

Southgate Street Brewery in the 1920s. The Southgate Street Brewery was closed in 1931 and later demolished in the 1960s to make way for the inner ring road as the main photograph shows.

1947
Tony Everard gains his fixed-wing pilot's licence.

1948
Tony Everard appointed as a Director of John Sarson & Son Ltd.

1948
End of wartime bread rationing.

1949
Death of Sir Lindsay Everard, son of Thomas William Everard.

1949
Tony Everard appointed as Chairman of Everards Brewery Ltd and John Sarson & Son Ltd.

1949
Harry Jarratt appointed to the Board of Directors.

1950
The Everards Quarter Century Club is formed.

1952
Death of George VI. Elizabeth II accedes to the throne.

1952
Birth of Serena Ann Spencer, daughter of Bettyne (née Everard) and Peter Spencer.

1953
Coronation of Queen Elizabeth II coincides with first ascent of Everest.

Everards Brewery Ltd

The Trent Brewery in its heyday.
The brewing process was labour intensive with fermenting vessels having to be painstakingly cleaned by hand between brews. The brewery had its own coopers to manufacture and maintain wooden casks.

In 1936 the company was renamed Everards Brewery Ltd, a successful share issue reflecting the performance of the company. Subscribers varied from individuals like Thomas James Morgan, who purchased ten shares, to blue-chip companies like the Prudential Assurance Co Ltd, which bought 22,500. Certificates were also issued to William Henry Hubbard, brewer, who bought 5400, William Spriggs Hubbard, brewer, who bought 800 and Florence Muriel Everard, widow, who bought 2000.

Sales at the brewery had recovered from the effects of the Depression of the early thirties, and it was a good time to invest. The economy of the country was picking up again as the slow process of rearmament gathered pace, and the European powers prepared themselves for the second great war of the 20th Century. Bill Hubbard Snr. had been joined at the company by his son Bill Hubbard Jnr., who would eventually succeed him as Managing Director. The two years before the war were spent expanding the distribution depot at Southgate Street to include a new bottling installation and a soft drinks hall.

The outbreak of war in September 1939 again brought rationing and shortages. For brewers this meant cuts in supplies of raw materials, especially hops which were grown in areas that lay easily within the range of the German bombers. To raise funds the government increased excise duty threefold in the first year, almost tripling the price of a pint by the end of the war. Conscription had been reintroduced in May, and for most of the next six years, the company had to operate on a skeleton staff with as few as three men running the Leicester operation for much of the war.

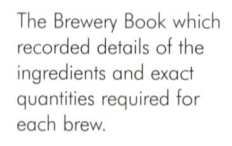

The Brewery Book which recorded details of the ingredients and exact quantities required for each brew.

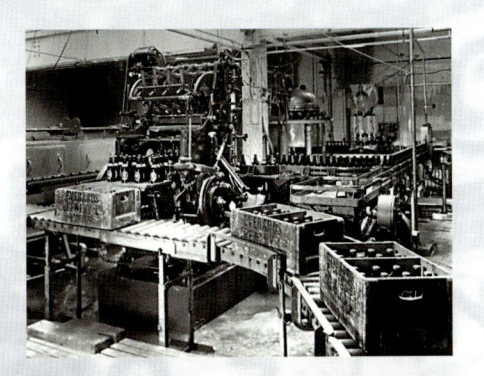

Above:
Southgate Street was a hive of activity with the installation of a new bottling hall and soft drinks plant.

Right, Top to Bottom:
Pubs added to the estate included The Heathcote Arms at Croft, The Free Trade Inn at Sileby and The Rose and Crown at Thurnby.

1953
John Sarson & Son (Loughborough) Ltd formed to cope with the expanding business of John Sarson & Son Ltd.

1954
Death of Bill Hubbard Snr.. Bill Hubbard Jnr. appointed Managing Director.

1954
Roger Bannister breaks four minute mile.

1954
Birth of Richard, son of Bettyne (née Everard) and Peter Spencer.

1954
Death of Florence Muriel Everard, wife of Thomas Everard.

1955
Commercial TV starts broadcasting in Britain.

1956
'Rock and roll' is the dance of the day.

1957
Leicester University is founded.

1957
Harold Weston joins the Everards board as a non-executive director.

1957
Space satellite 'Sputnik 1' launched by Soviet Union.

39

Patrick Anthony William Beresford Everard

Sir Lindsay had been ill for much of the war, and he was eventually forced to retire from active politics in 1945. Sadly, he was never to recover full health again and he died in Torquay in 1949 at the age of fifty-eight. The responsibility for running the company now fell upon the shoulders of the fourth generation of the family, Sir Lindsay's twenty-seven year old son, Tony Everard.

Like his father, Tony Everard had first chosen a career in the army and, after leaving Eton, had attended the Royal Military Academy at Sandhurst in Berkshire. In 1941, at the age of nineteen, he took a Regular Commission with the Royal Horse Guards. Serving as a Captain, he was wounded in action in 1944 while serving in Normandy after the D-Day landings but rejoined his regiment in the same year. In 1947 he resigned his Commission and joined the family company on the 14th of October.

Following in the footsteps of his father, grandfather and great-grandfather, Tony Everard took his public responsibilities very seriously, serving as a Rural District Councillor for Barrow on Soar for twenty-five years and becoming High Sheriff of Leicestershire in 1964.

The Fourth Generation.
Tony Everard (Born 1922).

Tony Everard, a man of action and sporting ability, who followed the family tradition of always combining his business career with service to the community.

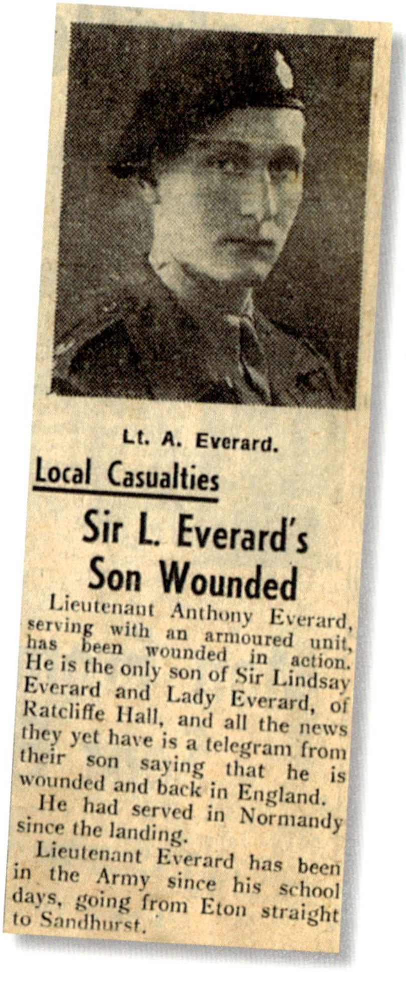

Tony Everard competes at the Prescott Hill Climb in his Aston Martin DB3S.

Lt. A. Everard.
Local Casualties
Sir L. Everard's Son Wounded

Lieutenant Anthony Everard, serving with an armoured unit, has been wounded in action. He is the only son of Sir Lindsay Everard and Lady Everard, of Ratcliffe Hall, and all the news they yet have is a telegram from their son saying that he is wounded and back in England.

He had served in Normandy since the landing.

Lieutenant Everard has been in the Army since his school days, going from Eton straight to Sandhurst.

A champion of youth and sporting ability, he identified the emerging talent of many local individuals, including Olympic Sailing Silver Medallist, John Merricks, and contributed to the development of their successful careers. He also supported many local sporting organisations with donations of equipment and finance and in 1978 created the family charitable trust 'The Everard Foundation.'

Tony inherited his father's love of flying and earned his fixed-wing pilot's licence in 1947. He was to become better known, however, for his passion for a new form of aviation – helicopters – and acquired his helicopter licence in 1963. In 1966 he founded the Helicopter Club of Great Britain and opened a heliport at Ratcliffe which hosted the club's first ever 'hover-in' the following year. His work in the organisation of the British Helicopter Championships was marked by the award of the Paul Tissandier Diploma in 1976 by the Fédération Aéronautique Internationale.

He often used helicopters on company business and when he flew in to the opening of new Everards pubs he certainly drew attention to the occasion! The Airman's Rest Hotel, Leicester Forest East was specifically designed to welcome fliers, and the landing area earned it the nickname 'The Hoteliport'.

The emblem of the Helicopter Club of Great Britain, founded by Tony Everard in 1966.

Tony Everard presents Leicestershire St. John Ambulance with a new mini bus.

The Swallow, Thurnby. Opened in 1964, it was the first pub built by Everards to include its own restaurant (and helicopter parking space!).

1959
First section of M1 opens.

1960
First working laser produced in the USA.

1961
Yuri Gagarin becomes the first man in space.

1962
Telstar satellite launched.

1963
The Beatles pop group wins international fame.

1963
Tony Everard gains his helicopter pilot's licence.

1964
Tony Everard appointed as High Sheriff of Leicestershire.

1965
Oil and gas found in the North Sea.

1966
Tony Everard opens a heliport at Ratcliffe.

1966
The twist and mini-skirts are high fashion.

1967
Death of Lady Everard, wife of Sir Lindsay Everard.

1967
World's first heart transplant takes place in South Africa.

1968
Oliver Steel joins the Board as a non-executive director.

Excellence through Independence

A board meeting in the Centenary Year 1949.
Present are Tony Everard, Bill Hubbard Snr., Bill Hubbard Jnr.,
Bill Frearson and Harry Jarratt.

Tony Everard participating in the new sport of heli-skiing.

Motorcycling – an abiding passion.

Tony Everard was also active in the field of motorsport, with a passion for both cars and motorcycles. He encouraged the foundation of the Donington 100 Motorcycle Group and participated in the revival of this famous Leicestershire circuit. On the race track he was easily identified by his distinctive number plates. He inherited Sir Lindsay's registration number AY2, which in 1903 was the first car number registered in Leicestershire. (Cars it transpired had even numbers whilst motorcycles had odd numbers.) Out of interest he tracked down AY1 to a wrecked motorcycle and acquired it, later adding AY3 and UT1, 2 and 3 to his collection.

As a dedicated skier, he founded the 'B and B' ('Black and Blue') ski club at St. Moritz. Even though the club was comprised of expert skiers, the emphasis was on fun, and one of the events was an egg-and-spoon race on skis.

A life-long squash player and coach, he represented Leicestershire and in 1979 reached the semi-finals of the British Vintage Squash Championships. On the threshold of his sixties he took up rowing and was instrumental in founding the National Rowing Centre at Holme Pierrepoint.

Tony Everard with his revolutionary gull-winged Mercedes outside Ratcliffe Hall in 1955.

42

When he joined the company in 1947, Tony Everard followed established industry practice and was seconded to another brewery, Lacon's in Great Yarmouth, to learn the craft and skills of the trade. On his return he was appointed first as a director of Everards Brewery Ltd. and then of John Sarson & Son Ltd, before taking up the Chairmanship of both companies on the death of his father.

During that time the business was being managed by Bill Hubbard Snr., Managing Director, assisted by his son, Bill Hubbard Jnr.. Despite the difficulties caused by post-war shortages (rationing did not end until 1954), Everards had been performing well, and sales in the year 1943-44 had reached a record peak when output climbed to 62,178 barrels. It was a time when many breweries were swallowed up by predators and many established names were lost forever, but during this period Tony Everard was resolute that the long-term interests of the staff and shareholders would be best served by maintaining the family company's independence.

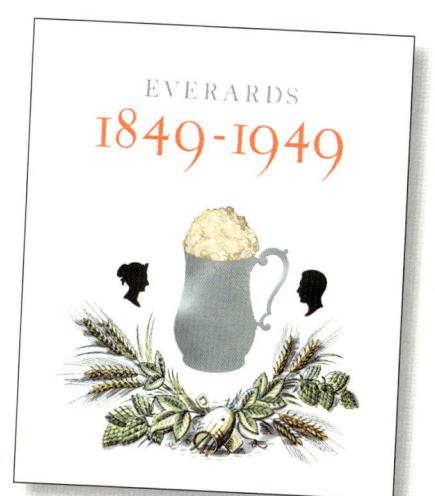

Above: Everards 100th Anniversary was marked by the production of a commemorative booklet.

Above Left: Delivering the ale. Brewing has always been as much a craft as an industry, with every job containing specialist knowledge vital to the final product.

Above: Bill Hubbard Jnr. worked for Everards for 45 years.

Below: Everards off-licences sold a vast range of products including draught beer.

1969
Neil Armstrong becomes the first man to set foot on the moon.

1970
Trent Brewery renamed as the Tiger Brewery.

1970
Silicon chip invented in the United States.

1971
Decimal currency introduced.

1971
Bill Hubbard retires after 17 years as Managing Director and becomes Vice Chairman.

1971
Duncan Bodger appointed Technical Director.

1971
New oil-fired boilers fitted in the Tiger Brewery to replace the old coal-fired ones.

1971
USSR soft lands space capsule on Mars.

1972
Anthony Morse becomes Managing Director.

1972
Ugandan Asians expelled – flee to United Kingdom.

1972
Tony Everard announces that his 18-year old nephew, Richard, will be joining the firm.

1972
Richard Everard commissioned from The Royal Military Academy, Sandhurst into the Blues and Royals.

43

'A Family Firm'

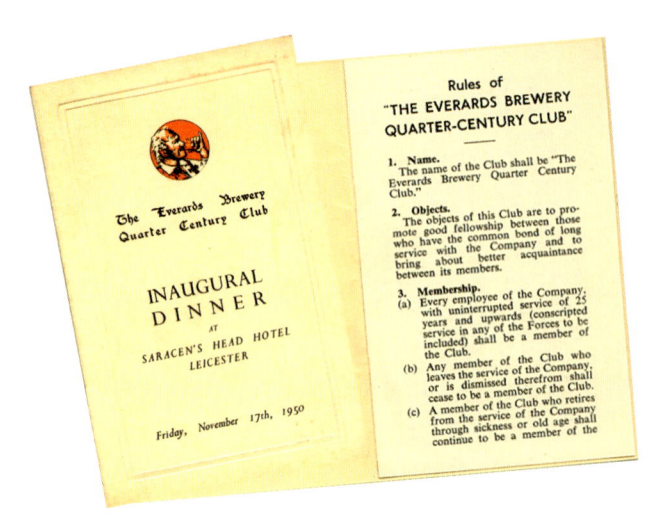

As a family business, Tony Everard placed great importance upon staff job satisfaction, regarding this as one of Everards prime strengths. Long service, always a feature of the company, was recognised more formally in 1950 with the inauguration of the Quarter Century Club, an association for all staff who had completed twenty-five years service with Everards.

The first meeting on the 17th November 1950 was marked with a celebration dinner at the Saracen's Head, an Everards public house since 1897. The first member was the Managing Director, William Henry Hubbard, who had reached his fifty-first year of service having joined in 1899 under Tony Everard's grandfather Thomas.

In his address Tony Everard said: 'Despite the fact that we are a small concern (for the present) and do not employ large numbers, there are here tonight 32 men whose total service at present amounts to over 1,000 years. I wonder why in particular have we been so fortunate over these past 100 years. Mainly I think, because we are a family business, that is a business run by one particular family, and whose staff become virtually a family also, joined in the smooth running of day-to-day affairs.'

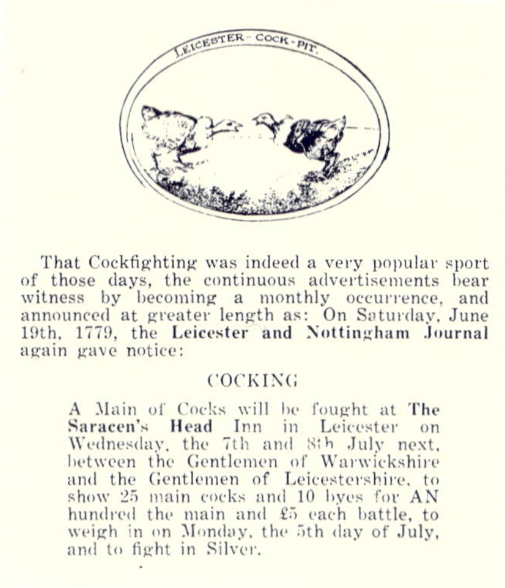

The Saracen's Head, Hotel Street, Leicester where a pub has been situated since the 14th Century. During the 18th Century it was a renowned cockfighting venue – a popular sport at the time.
In 1950 the Saracen's Head was the venue for the inaugural dinner of Everards Quarter Century Club. In 1996 it became Molly O'Grady's, the pub at the heart of the Irish community in Leicester.

The Everards Sports and Social Club Annual Dinner, March 1955.

Everards Centenary Dinner & Dance, 6th December 1949 at the De Montfort Hall.

The social life of the company was always very active, and during this time the highlight of each year was undoubtedly the annual dinner dance held in the De Montfort Hall. Staff and guests would enjoy an excellent dinner before taking to the dance floor accompanied by the music of famous bandleaders like Joe Loss and Victor Sylvester. These events were organised by Bill Lofthouse who had joined the company in the same year as Tony Everard. A local personality, and a toastmaster in his spare time, he was responsible for the formation of various clubs and societies including the Everards Sports and Social Club. He was also asked to become the first editor of the company journal 'Tiger Talk'.

'…we are a family business…whose staff become virtually a family also.'

Tiger Talk, the Everards Company Journal, first appeared in 1972 and has been a feature of company life ever since.

Victor Sylvester and guests at the Everards Sports and Social Club Annual Ball in the 1950s.

1972
Tigers Head logo and Tiger Special Keg introduced.

1972
Lovett Bros. Soft Drinks acquired.

1972
Everards Mild wins the Bronze Medal at the International Brewing, Bottling and Allied Trades Exhibition.

1972
47 day coal miners' strike cripples Britain.

1973
UK joins Common Market.

1973
Bill Hubbard Jnr. retires as Vice Chairman.

1973
Harold Weston retires from the Board.

1973
Everards installs its first computer, an ICL 1901A.

1974
Two General Elections take place in the wake of the miners' strike.

1974
Everards Brewery's 125th Anniversary.

1974
Sabre Lager is introduced.

1974
Peter Stephens joins the board as Financial Director.

1975
Oliver Steel retires from the Board, and Adrian Weston joins as a non-executive director.

A Time of Change

The landlord of The Globe was well known for flower displays (above) in the late 1940s, while The Antelope in Silver Street (below) featured murals of Greek scenes.

Packaging design came about in the desire for more competitive marketing, and the face of Everards ales began changing regularly to keep pace with contemporary design.

With the daily management of the company in good hands, Tony Everard concentrated his attentions on the pub estate. He was a regular visitor to Everards establishments, meeting tenants and managers and discussing the opportunities for business enhancement and development.

Everards pubs were now amongst the best run and most successful in the land, and the company was well equipped to supply all their needs direct from the brewery. The beer, wines and spirits, soft drinks, cigarettes and even the matches all travelled on the Everards drays. Tony Everard, however, saw that times were changing. He recognised that pubs, traditionally a male domain, offered the opportunity to provide a more enlightened and comfortable atmosphere in which women, and ultimately families, could feel both welcome and relaxed.

The post-war world was a quite different place to the society of the 1930s. Social conventions were relaxing, and leisure opportunities were opening up as society gradually became more youth-orientated and the pace of life increased. Everards were in the vanguard of the recognition of a more family and consumer orientated public house. A programme of significant capital investment was initiated, and the estate quickly began to change.

Women began to feel more comfortable in what was traditionally seen as a male environment.

Tony Everard's strategy was to develop the idea of Everards 'Friendly Inns'. Pubs were modernised to 'look like your front room'; the decor and furnishings were of a high standard; interiors were upgraded, including the extensive use of warm, wood panelling; new facilities were added, with some pubs even having proper dance floors installed.

The Friendly Inns were a great success, attracting more women and families, and fulfilling Everards ambition to own and operate one of the best pub estates in Britain.

Adding new pubs to the estate was increasingly difficult. Pubs rarely came onto the market, not least because breweries were wary of losing an outlet to a competitor. For a long time it was equally difficult to get licensing approval for extensions to existing premises, and seeking new licences was so difficult that it could take ten years or more to reach a conclusion. However, in the 1960s the construction of the Leicester inner ring road saw many old pubs demolished, and this time of change gave Everards the opportunity to build several new pubs in a 'ring' around the city.

Celebrating the Coronation of Queen Elizabeth II in 1953.

Society gradually became more youth-orientated!

'Pubs were modernised to look like your front room.'

Many new pubs established their trade in the 1960s, like The Tom Thumb at Blaby, The Winstanley at Braunstone (below) and The Firs at Wigston.

1975
The kegging plant is moved from Leicester to Burton.

1976
£2,000,000 is invested into a programme of upgrading the pub estate.

1976
Worst drought in the UK for 200 years.

1976
Tony Everard awarded the Paul Tissandier Diploma.

1977
Richard Everard leaves the army and joins Everards.

1977
USA space shuttle *Enterprise* makes its first manned flight.

1978
Everards Brewery Ltd. purchases 24 pubs from the Ruddles Brewery for £730,000.

1978
Tony Everard becomes Everards first company president, and Oliver Steel returns as company chairman.

1978
Computerised order system introduced at Everards.

1978
Everards ceases the bottling of its own beers and soft drinks.

1978
Tony Everard sets up the Everard Foundation, the charitable trust of the Everard family.

47

Excellence through Independence

'… by 1967 the company was operating 125 pubs and hotels and 40 off-licences…'

Everards memorabilia from the 1960s.

Right and above: The Shakespeare in Braunstone was converted from five old cottages by Everards in 1954. In August 1991 it was closed for a year by extensive fire damage.

The 1950s and 1960s were a time of steady expansion for Everards as the company accelerated its programme of refurbishing existing properties and creating new pubs, like the Shakespeare in Braunstone and The Firs at Wigston. The policy was far-sighted and very effective, and by 1967 the company was operating 125 pubs and hotels and 40 off-licences. Everards had also become a major employer with nearly seven hundred staff working in the public houses, brewery, offices and warehouses.

The Managing Director during this period of achievement was Bill Hubbard Jnr., who had been appointed following the death of his father in 1954. He was joined three years later by Harold Weston, a local solicitor, as a non-executive director. Other board changes included Oliver Steel who joined from Courage in 1968. In 1972 Anthony Morse took over as Managing Director with Bill Hubbard Jnr. becoming Vice Chairman before retiring from this position in 1973.

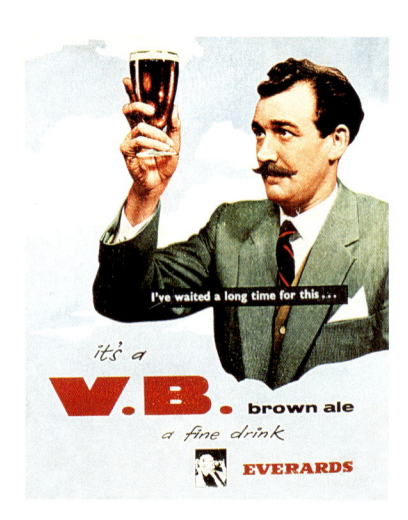

Above: The Firs, Wigston.

The Everards Tiger

The decades after World War II had seen the growth of an increasingly competitive market place, and more emphasis began to be placed by the brewing industry upon advertising, marketing and developing brand identities. Reflecting the new tastes which emerged in this era of change, the traditional draught milds and bitters of Everards range were now joined by some new 'bright' or 'keg' ales. These complemented the range of bottled beers which ranged from Amberlite, a 'light dinner ale', to Stag Stout.

Everards keg beer was sold first as Golden Ale, and then as Crown Keg, but in 1970 the decision was made to launch a new keg product with a brand new image. In August 1972 the first barrels of Everards Tiger Special Keg were delivered to pubs, and a new age in beer drinking was born.

The new ale was given a distinctive presence on the bar through an orange and black striped font, reflecting a new corporate image for the company centred on the Tiger's Head logo. The Tiger has a special significance in Leicester as the Leicestershire regiment were nicknamed 'The Tigers' because of their length of service in India. The name has also become associated with the city's highly successful rugby club. The Everards Tiger was a bright, modern image which symbolised the progressive and confident mood of the company at the start of a new decade.

Above: The changing face of the Everards Tiger throughout the years.

Left: The brewery took every opportunity to promote Tiger, including using the buildings at Castle Street as advertising hoardings!

1979
Old Original Strong Traditional Ale introduced.

1979
Everards subcontract their deliveries to Podgers Brothers, a local haulage contractor and family business.

1979
The 134 acre Grove Farm estate at Narborough is bought for £500,000.

1979
Richard Everard joins Everards Managed House Department.

1979
Margaret Thatcher becomes Britain's first woman Prime Minister.

1980
Everards begin exporting cans of Old Original to France.

1981
Tony Everard cuts the first turf at the Castle Acres development.

1981
Everards Brewery appointed as sole agents for Tuborg in the Midlands.

1981
Marriage of Lady Diana Spencer and Prince Charles.

1981
Maiden voyage of the space shuttle *Columbia*.

1981
Richard Everard marries Caroline Hill.

1982
Argentina invades the Falkland Islands – recaptured in ten weeks.

49

New Tastes for New Times

The advertising acted like a beacon for Beacon.

'Whatever you say, say it with Sabre.'

Sabre Lager was an outstanding success for the brewery in the 1970s.

The success of Tiger Bitter was followed by the launch of a lighter product, christened Beacon Bitter by Harry Jarratt, after Leicestershire's highest landmark, Beacon Hill in Bradgate Park. Like Tiger, Beacon soon established itself in bars and off-licences. It proved particularly popular in the five-pint cans that became a feature of every good party in the early 1970s.

Always alive to changing customer tastes, Tony Everard watched the emergence of the draught lager market with great interest. He decided that if the public were looking for lager, then Everards would meet their demands by introducing their own brand. In June 1974 the company launched Sabre Lager, a product which was top fermented like an ale. An advertising campaign was launched with the catch phrase: 'Whatever you say, say it with Sabre.'

At its peak, Sabre Lager was responsible for a quarter of the company's total beer sales. However, throughout the wider market, national and international brands were beginning to make their mark and, in 1981, production of Sabre finished when Everards won the Tuborg Lager franchise for the Midlands.

The ever increasing demand for these new products pushed the production facilities to their limits and a new, upgraded kegging plant was installed at Burton, with the head office and bottling remaining at Castle Street in Leicester.

The Sun Inn at Cottesmore was one of over twenty pubs purchased from Ruddles Brewery in 1978.

Phil Fox (right), a lifetime regular at The Cradock, was quick to recognise the value of collecting beer memorabilia. He is seen here displaying some of his Everards items with Chris Faircliffe, Everards Managing Director, Trading.

In 1974, Everards 125th Anniversary was celebrated with a dinner-dance for twelve hundred guests at the De Montfort Hall. The company, however, was already planning for the future with new products, new markets and new pubs like the Honeycomb and the Ferrers Arms, both in Derbyshire.

In 1978, whilst Anthony Morse was Managing Director, an acquisition of over twenty pubs from the Ruddles Brewery increased the number of premises to a new high of one hundred and fifty. The following year the range of ales was completed when Mild, Beacon and Tiger were joined by a new, strong, traditional ale called Old Original. This was the first Everards ale to be advertised on television and used a commercial which featured Bill Maynard, a local actor and personality from Sapcote.

There were changes in the boardroom too. In 1978 Oliver Steel took over as Chairman, and Tony Everard became the first ever Company President, after almost thirty years in the hot seat.

Old Original joins the line up of Everards fine beers in 1979.

To celebrate the Silver Jubilee of Queen Elizabeth II in 1977, Everards produced a commemorative ale.

Above: The Fox and Goose at Illston on the Hill as it was in 1978 when it was purchased from Ruddles. The Fox and Goose is Everards smallest pub.

Left: Bill Maynard featured in the company's first TV commercial.

1982
Castle Acres offices, warehouse and processing area are officially opened.

1982
Old Original is advertised on television during the football World Cup.

1982
Old Original wins the gold medal in the strong ale class and the Supreme Championship Gold Medal at the 1982 London Beer Festival.

1983
The Castle Street site is sold.

1983
Richard Everard joins the Everards Board as Commercial Director.

1983
The Falkland Islands Brewery in Port Stanley opens.

1984
Adrian Weston replaces Oliver Steel as Company Chairman.

1984
Phase 1 of the new Castle Acres brewhouse begins.

1984
Nicholas Lloyd joins Everards from Grand Metropolitan.

1985
Castle Acres brewhouse is opened by Nigel Lawson, MP for Blaby and Chancellor of the Exchequer.

1985
The Tiger Brewery in Burton is sold to the National Brewery Museum Trust.

1985
Everards acquire Rutland Vintners.

Castle Acres

The new brewery at Castle Acres, opened in 1985. Its capacity was increased in two subsequent phases of development.

> '…a new brewhouse, which would incorporate the best of traditional and new technology, was planned.'

Tony Everard cuts the first turf at Castle Acres in 1981.

The fermentation vessels were lifted into the brewery by two cranes.

The continuing growth of the business placed increasing pressure on the facilities in Castle Street. The old brewery had been demolished to make way for the construction of the long-awaited inner ring road. In 1979 the company bought 134 acres at Grove Farm, near to the M1, with a plan to build a new office and distribution complex. This was to be named Castle Acres after the old offices in Castle Street.

In 1981 Tony Everard cut the first turf at the new site, and eighteen months later the new office building was ready for occupation and the new warehouse and distribution centre ready to take in its first stock. Staff pulled out all the stops to allow the smooth transfer of more than 1,000 tons of office equipment in just over two days. The company computer – the lifeline which handled all accounts, orders and company data – was disconnected, transported and reinstalled, all within twenty-four hours. John Sarson & Son vacated their warehouse at Murrayfield Road, and distribution of wine and spirits began from Castle Acres.

Everards was one of the first companies to recognise the benefits of a location close to the motorway network.

All Everards ales continued to be produced at the Tiger Brewery in Burton, with some notable successes. At the 1982 London Beer Festival, Old Original won not only the gold medal for the best brew in the strong ale class, but also the Supreme Championship Gold Medal in competition with 70 individual brews, entered by 49 different brewers.

The old Victorian Burton brewery, however, was now over one hundred years old and would have needed a huge investment if it were to keep pace with modern demands. For economic, organisational and structural reasons, it made sense to centralise operations at Castle Acres and so a new brewhouse, which would incorporate the best of tradition and new technology, was planned.

On the 29th March 1985 the Chancellor of the Exchequer, Nigel Lawson, MP for Blaby, officially opened Phase 1 of the new brewhouse: it had an initial capacity that enabled it to brew 12,500 barrels of Old Original per annum. At the same time The National Brewery Museum Trust was formed to acquire the Victorian Tiger Brewery and to operate it as Britain's only working brewery museum. Everards awarded the Trust a fixed-term contract to continue to brew the company's ales, which would allow the Trust time to develop their own markets.

Above: Old Original won the gold medal at the 1982 London Beer Festival.

Above Left: Chancellor of the Exchequer Nigel Lawson toasted the opening of Phase 1 of the Castle Acres brewhouse with the first pint of Old Original.

The age of computers began to influence everything from brewing to sales.

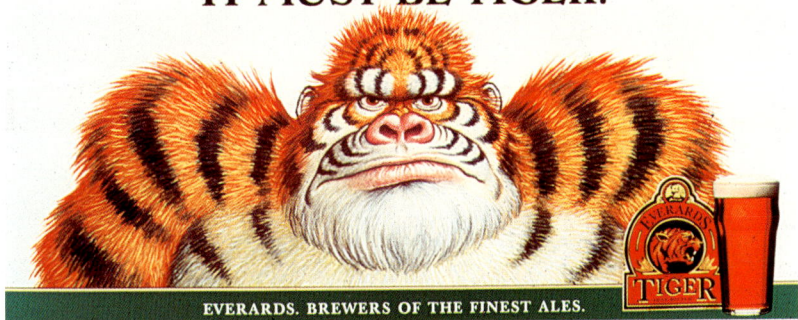

Tiger advertising became more distinctive and began to reflect the personality of the brand.

1985
Nicholas Lloyd joins the Board as Retail Director.

1986
Richard Everard becomes Vice-Chairman.

1986
Old Original Beer Bread launched with Charles Geary and Sons.

1986
Everards Developments Ltd. open Caroline Court named after Caroline, Richard Everard's wife.

1987
Anthony Morse retires as Managing Director.

1987
Nicholas Lloyd appointed Group Managing Director.

1987
Phase 2 of the Castle Acres brewhouse completed.

1988
Richard Everard becomes Chairman on 1st January.

1988
The Founders Head logo is introduced.

1988
Everards Brewery Ltd. is separated into two distinct trading divisions – Retail and Wholesale.

1988
The launch of 'Original Inns' begins a period of heavy investment in Everards pub estate.

1989
Death of Bettyne Spencer, daughter of Sir Lindsay Everard.

Excellence through Independence

'For the first time since 1892 all of Everards beer production was once again being carried out in Leicester.'

Above: Castle Acres combined the best of new technology with the best of brewing tradition.

Right: Pick up a Penguin.
The Globe Hotel in Port Stanley was an Everards pub. Everards provided the Falkland Islands with its first brewery when it opened in 1983.

By August 1987 Phase 2 had been completed, raising capacity to 28,500 barrels and incorporating production of Beacon Bitter. In February 1990 Phase 3 brought production capacity up to nearly 70,000 barrels with Tiger Best Bitter and Everards Mild completing the portfolio at Castle Acres. The contract with the old Tiger Brewery finished and the company's association with Burton-upon-Trent ended after almost a century. For the first time since 1892 all of Everards beers were once again being brewed in Leicester.

Castle Acres was not the only new brewery initiated by Everards in the 1980s. In 1982 Anthony Morse became the first British businessman to visit the Falkland Islands after the conflict, and the result was the formation of a new company, Everards Brewery (Falkland Islands) Ltd. On the 25th February 1983 Sir Rex Hunt, the Governor, formally opened the new brewery. The plant had a capacity of forty barrels a week and produced a cask-conditioned beer called Penguin Ale, a name chosen by the islanders themselves. Sadly, as the garrison declined the project proved uneconomic and the brewery was decommissioned in 1986.

During the late eighties, with the country in recession and the brewing industry in general suffering from massive over-capacity, the company continued to develop strategies to identify new markets and to maximise its assets. Sales of cask-conditioned beers were growing steadily, and the pub estate was expanded into London with the purchase of the Radnor Arms in Kensington.

In 1984 Oliver Steel retired and Adrian Weston became Chairman. In 1985 Nicholas Lloyd was brought onto the Board as Retail Director, and two years later he took over as Group Managing Director on the retirement of Anthony Morse.

On the 1st January 1988, Richard Everard, the fifth generation of the Everards Brewery family, was appointed Chairman. His connection with the company dated back to 1972 when Tony Everard, a bachelor, announced that his eighteen year-old nephew would be joining the firm after serving in the army.

The Radnor Arms, Warwick Road, Kensington. Everards most southerly and sole London pub.

The Cherry Tree, Little Bowden, acquired as a leasehold in 1972 and purchased in 1981.

WE'LL REMAIN INDEPENDENT SAYS BREWERY CHAIRMAN

A FIRM assurance that Everards Brewery will remain an independent company and that provision has been made for this plan, was given by Mr. Anthony Everard, chairman, speaking at the annual dinner of the brewery's sports and social club, last night.

Stressing that the company will go "on and on and on" he said that the only problem that they could have got into was through death duties. He recalled that the family were caught by terrible death duties some years ago and since then they had been quite determined to stand by the firm and ensure that the family business should not die.

"In November last year certain papers were signed which make the company 100 per cent safe if I should die," he added.

He went on to explain that his nephew, 18-year-old Mr. Richard Spencer, had changed his name to Everard in November last year and after serving a three-year spell with the Army he would be joining the firm.

MR. RICHARD EVERARD

Richard Everard commits to joining the company.

Nicholas Lloyd was appointed Group Managing Director in 1987, having originally joined the management team in 1984.

1989
Tony Everard awarded the Breguet Trophy.

1989
Everards acquire Central Wines of Oadby and the old-established business of Patens Wines Ltd. of Peterborough.

1989
Fall of the Berlin Wall.

1990
Phase 3 of the Castle Acres brewhouse completed.

1990
Mrs Serena Richards, sister of Richard Everard, joins the Board as a non-executive director.

1990
Tiger Best Bitter gets a distinctive new brand image.

1990
Beacon Bitter wins a gold medal at The Brewing Industry International Awards Competition at Burton.

1990
Computer simulation (virtual reality) created in the USA.

1991
The Everards Company Philosophy is published.

1991
Death of Phyllis Logan née Everard, sister of Sir Lindsay Everard.

1991
New branding for Old Original and Beacon Bitter is introduced.

1991
End of Gulf War.

55

Richard Anthony Spencer Everard, D.L.

The Fifth Generation.
Richard Everard (Born 1954).

Richard Everard with his wife Caroline, and children Charlotte and Julian.

Everards 150th Anniversary provided an opportunity for Richard Everard to research both family and brewery history.

Richard Everard attended Eton College where he continued the family's sporting tradition by playing football, cricket, rugby and Eton Fives at the highest level for the school. He then went on to the Royal Military Academy at Sandhurst, where he was sent on a winter warfare course with the Norwegian army, learning Arctic survival and combat techniques. He was commissioned into the Blues and Royals at Windsor in 1973 and during the next five years served in England, Northern Ireland, Germany, Norway, Denmark, Cyprus, Turkey, Greece and Jamaica. He also played rugby, cricket and skied for his regimental teams.

On 9th May 1981 he married Caroline Anne Hill and they have two children – Charlotte, born in 1985, and Julian who was born two years later.

Serena, Richard's sister, trained as a professional florist, working with Constance Spry. In 1978 she married Charles Richards, a great friend of Richard's since their time at Sandhurst together, and they have three boys, Edward, Jamie and Harry. In 1990 Richard asked her to join the board as a non-executive director, in which capacity she has been a valuable member of the team.

Richard Everard during his service with the Blues and Royals.

Following the tradition of four generations of Everards, Richard has also become involved in public and charitable organisations and projects. As well as his commitments to national brewery associations he is very involved with the Institute of Directors, Leicester Promotions, is President of Age Concern Leicestershire and is a Trustee of the Leicestershire Police Charitable Trust. In 1997 he was invited to become a Deputy Lieutenant for Leicestershire.

Richard is also a trustee of the Everard Foundation, which since its inception has donated in excess of £400,000 to a multitude of charitable causes, including the gift of the 'sensory perception unit' at The Rainbows Hospice near Loughborough.

A keen sportsman since his days at Eton, Richard now enjoys tennis, golf and skiing. Like his grandfather, Sir Lindsay, he is at home in the country, enjoying fieldsports with his working gun dog, Storm. Although he served in the Household Cavalry, he much prefers his horsepower to be vehicular, passing his Advanced Driving Test at the age of eighteen, before adding tank, motorcycle and helicopter licences later on. Indeed, on HRH The Duke of York's 16th birthday he taught His Royal Highness to drive a light tank in Windsor Great Park.

Richard Everard and Serena Richards, representing The Everard Foundation, present Leicestershire's Chief Constable with two patrol cars to be used for community policing.

Richard Everard flies in to the site of the new Rainbows Hospice near Loughborough with a cheque for £20,000.

Everards became the first British brewer to sponsor a TV programme with Central TV's 'Central Match Live.'

In 1993 Carling was added to Everards lager portfolio.

1991
Dissolution of the USSR.

1992
Everards acquire nine pubs from Whitbread.

1992
The Everards Brewery Visitor Centre is opened at Castle Acres.

1992
Everards Brewery wins the Leicestershire Business Challenge Award.

1992
Beacon Bitter and Old Original both win awards at Brewing Industry International Awards Competition.

1992
Richard Everard appointed as Chairman of the Leicester Institute of Directors and President of Age Concern Leicester.

1993
Carling and Labatt's are added to Everards lager portfolio.

1993
Everards become the first British brewer to sponsor a TV programme with Central TV's 'Central Match Live.'

1993
'Daredevil', a new winter warmer, is introduced.

1994
The Everards Environmental Policy Group is formed.

1994
Tiger Best Bitter launched into the national market through a new National Accounts team.

Excellence through Independence

Richard Everard 'rolls out the barrel' as he learns all about the family business during his training.

'...Everards became a wholly private company once more.'

Ivan Ball – the first Everards licensee to receive an MBE.

Everards won the Leicestershire Business Challenge in 1992.

The Everards Retirement Association was set up to provide support and assistance for former Everards employees in later life.

After leaving the army, Richard joined Everards Brewery Ltd. on the 11th July 1977. He spent a year at the Horselydown Brewery in London training as a brewer, including delivering beer on the drays and running one of the Courage hop farms during the picking season. He sat the Brewers Society Licencees course before spending a year with Bass gaining experience in their public house division. In 1979, after almost two years intensive training across the brewing industry, he returned to Leicester to take up the post of District Manager in the Managed House Department.

Keen to develop formally his commercial awareness, Richard undertook training which led to the 'Institute of Directors Diploma in Company Direction' in 1986. It was this insight into the IOD that led him into closer involvement with them, sitting on the Council for two years before joining the Professional Standards Committee, whose remit it is to increase the professionalism of all active practising directors.

In 1981, reflecting the importance of property to the company, he went to work in the City of London with Rowe & Pitman Property Services, a commercial property firm. On his return the company had moved into their new headquarters at Castle Acres, a project that Richard had worked on during his spell in London. He was appointed as Commercial Director of Everards on the 1st October 1983, and his new role saw him dealing with the company's portfolio of unlicenced property, including the project that saw the creation of the Fosse Park shopping centre. He became Vice-Chairman in 1986, taking over as Chairman from Adrian Weston two years later.

A New Philosophy

Richard Everard and his management team, led by Nicholas Lloyd, began the new dynasty by undertaking a detailed appraisal of the business and the opportunities offered by a new climate of change in both the brewing and pub industries. This resulted in several exciting initiatives.

There was a vibrant, new corporate identity which emphasised the heritage of the company and featured the 'Founder's Head.' A new Company Philosophy was also established. This stated the principles on which the company would operate. Many of the ideals remained the same as those promoted by the Founder himself. These included the statement that Everards would remain 'an independent family business.' This was underpinned when the company bought back its remaining preference shares in 1997 to become a private company once more. Recognition of the value of the Philosophy was forthcoming when Everards won the Leicestershire Business Challenge in 1992 and then the Investors in People Award in 1998. Part of the prize from the former award allowed Everards to become one of the first Leicester businesses to establish a formal Environmental Management Policy.

Two new trading divisions, Retail and Wholesale, were created and a programme of pub property improvements, totalling nearly £20m during the late 80s and early 90s, capitalised upon the growing demand from families and business customers. There were major developments at many key pubs, including the launch of three new budget hotels to complement the facilities at The Red Cow, The Mill on the Soar and Bardon Hall (now The Charnwood Arms). It was an exciting time, and Everards were firmly at the forefront of pub retailing in the East Midlands.

The new 'Founder's Head' corporate identity.

Everards were quick to recognise the opportunities offered by budget hotels.

The expanding Everards estate includes pubs of unique character such as The Anne of Cleves, Melton Mowbray, a building originally gifted by Henry VIII to his estranged wife.

Everards celebrated recognition of their most valuable asset when the company received the Investors in People Award in 1998.

The Everards Company Philosophy.

1994
Beacon Bitter wins its class at the Champion Beer of Britain Competition at The Great British Beer Festival.

1994
Richard Everard appointed as Chairman of Leicester Promotions.

1994
Nelson Mandella becomes President of South Africa.

1994
IRA declares a ceasefire.

1995
The Everards estate reaches 150 with the acquisition of three new pubs, followed by a further five later in the year.

1997
Everards Brewery Ltd. becomes a wholly private concern again when the Preference Shares are bought in.

1997
Richard Everard appointed Deputy Lieutenant for Leicestershire.

1997
Death of Diana, Princess of Wales.

1998
Everards Brewery Ltd. receives the award of 'Investor in People'.

1998
'Tiger Mania' advertising is voted Top Trade Campaign of the year by leading trade publication 'Licensee and Morning Advertiser'.

1998
Everards bottled beers win three awards at The British Bottlers' Institute Ale & Lager Competition including a gold medal for Tiger Best Bitter.

Towards the Millennium

The Quay – a new £2 million development in the heart of Leicester.

Seasonal ales became a feature of the product range.

Above: Beacon Bitter won its class at the 1990 Brewing Industry International Awards and The 1994 CAMRA Champion Beer of Britain Competition.

Left: In 1998 'Tiger Mania' won Trade Advertising Campaign of the Year.

The return of all brewing to Leicester in 1990 proved extremely positive for Everards ales. Tiger Best Bitter, then Beacon, Old Original and finally Mild were given new looks. A new Free Trade National Accounts team was set up, and Everards traditional ales started to enjoy success throughout Britain. It also began a decade when Everards ales won many awards for their high quality, good presentation and distinctive marketing. In 1990 Beacon Bitter won its class at the Brewing Industry International Awards and then repeated this success at The 1994 CAMRA Champion Beer of Britain Competition. Old Original and Daredevil also tasted success whilst Tiger Best Bitter was awarded the Gold Medal at the BBI Ale and Lager Competition in 1998. In the same year it also received the accolade of Trade Advertising Campaign of the Year from 'Licensee and Morning Advertiser' for its eye-catching 'Tiger Mania' advertising.

Meanwhile the task of developing public houses, products and services was continuing apace. The boundaries of the pub estate were expanded into ten counties. There were also many refurbishments and developments to enhance and extend the facilities available to customers.

One of the most significant projects was the creation of The Quay. This £2 million investment saw the construction of a new pub inside the shell of a Victorian building on Bede Island at the heart of Leicester's city regeneration programme. The Quay was designed to combine the best of the old with the best of the new, an approach epitomised by Everards for five generations.

The Everards Board, March 1999. L to R: Richard Cave (Managing Director, Retail); Chris Faircliffe (Managing Director, Trading); Nicholas Lloyd (Group Managing Director); Richard Everard (Chairman); Serena Richards (Non-Executive Director); Mark Newman (Financial Director & Company Secretary); Adrian Weston (Non-Executive Director).

A Royal Beginning to the Next 150 Years

On 26th February 1999, HRH The Duke of Edinburgh visited Castle Acres and, after enjoying lunch in the brewery visitor centre, unveiled a plaque commemorating Everards first 150 years. He was introduced to every member of staff at the brewery and to long-serving pub tenants and managers. His visit celebrated the end of one era and the beginning of a new one; not just the end of the first 150 years but also the start of a new millennium.

What the next 150 years holds for Everards is difficult to predict. The pace of change is constantly accelerating, fuelled by the electronic age and the internet. Pubs and the companies which operate them are changing dramatically. Tony Everard's vision of creating family-friendly pubs has largely been realised, and the range of facilities on offer grows almost daily. Investment in pubs is at an all-time high as they compete in a dynamic and lucrative leisure and entertainment industry.

Against this ever-changing backdrop, the long-established Everards tradition of innovation and forward-thinking gives considerable cause for optimism, both now and for the future. A family business which has maintained its commercial independence whilst involving its staff, suppliers and customers in the spirit of a larger family surely has a winning formula. It is this formula and the pursuit of excellence through independence which will ensure the success of Everards for at least another 150 years.

Above: HRH The Duke of Edinburgh unveils a plaque commemorating Everards first 150 years.

Left: Everards traditional ales are enjoyed throughout the country.

Everards online. The Everards internet site allows beer lovers and pub goers throughout the world instant access to information about the company.

Above:
Tiger Triple Gold
– a new ale to commemorate Everards 150th Anniversary.

Left:
The Family Brewery –
Everards Staff,
February 1999.

The Everards Estate

Pub	Location	Traded From
Aberdale	Shackerdale Rd	1963
Admiral Beaty / Prince Blucher	152 Wellington St	1888
Admiral Nelson	14 Humberstone Gate	1895
Airman's / Airman's Rest	Ratby Lane	1941
Albion Vaults	Burton On Trent	1935
Anchor	Hartshill	1995
Anchor Hotel & Offices	Charles St	1926
Anne of Cleves	Melton	1995
Antelope	16 Silver St	1888
Ashby Woulds	Moira	1973
Bakers Arms	Friars Causeway	1884
Bakers Arms	126 Birstall St	1911
Balloon	Lutterworth	1972
Bandwagon / Loughborough Hotel	Loughborough	1923
Barley Mow	London Rd	1904
Barley Mow	Cadeby	1919
Barrel Inn	Bagworth	1911
Bat & Wickets	Bailiff St, Northampton	1973
Bath Hotel	7 Bath Lane	1887
Beaumanor Arms	Woodhouse	1899
Bedford	Leamington Spa	1995
Beeches	Wardens Walk	1970
Beeswing	Kettering	1968
Birch Tree Inn	Bardon	1921
Bishop Blaize	Loughborough	1953
Black Bull	Market Overton	1978
Black Horse	Aylestone	1896
Black Horse	Braunstone Gate	1934
Black Horse	Foxon St	1884
Black Lion	Belgrave Gate	1890
Black Swan Inn	Kilby	1919
Blackbird	Blackbird Rd	1939
Blue Bell	Stoney Stanton	1898
Blue Bell	Desford	1901
Blue Bell	Hoby	1912
Blue Boar	63 Southgate St	1895
Blues	Downing Drive	1976
Bradgate	Newtown Linford	1926
Brant Inn / Branting Hill Hotel	Groby	1946
Braunstone	Narborough Rd	1925
Brewers Arms	Belgrave Gate	1897
Bricklayers Arms	Thornton	1911
Bridle Lane Tavern	Junction Rd	1902
Britannia	10 Castle St	1894
Bull	Market Deeping	1978
Bulls Head	Cosby	1887
Bulls Head	Whetstone	1892
Bulls Head	Leicester Forest West	1897
Bulls Head	Ratby	1902
Bulls Head	Desford	1926
Bumper Inn	Carley St	1913
Burlington	46 Guthlaxton St	1886
Carington Arms*	Ashby Folville	1978
Carpenters Arms	Walesby	1992
Collyweston Slater / Cavalier	Collyweston	1995
Charnwood Arms / Bardon Hall	Coalville	1989
Cheney Arms	Gaddesby	1978
Cherry Tree	Little Bowden	1972
City & Counties Club	Peterborough	1996
City Arms	Saffron Lane	1925
Coach & Horses	Oxford St	1904
Coach & Horses	Markfield	1925
Coach & Horses	Lubenham	1975
Cotes Mill*	Loughborough	1992
County Arms	Cambridge	1992
County Arms / Union Inn	Blaby	1905
Cradock Arms	Knighton	1925
Cricketers / Cricket Ground Hotel	1 Grace Road, Aylestone	1900
Crown	Shepshed	1980

Pub	Location	Traded From
Crown & Dolphin	1 Holy Bones	1890
Crown & Thistle	Dunton Basset	1887
Crown Hotel	Uppingham	1978
Crown Inn	Melton Mowbray	1980
Crown Inn	Nottingham	1925
Crows Nest / Newfound Pool	King Richards Rd	1886
Dannett Tavern / Dannett Hall	62 Noble St	1925
Dog & Gun	Keyham	1938
Dog & Gun	Whetstone Gorse	1906
Dolphin Inn	East St, Stamford	1978
Dominion	Dominion Rd	1958
Dove	Downing Drive	1958
Dragon / George & Dragon	Newbold Verdon	1970
Duke of York	Southgate St	1907
Duke of York	Mountsorrel	1922
Durham Ox	Great Wigston	1920
Earl of Lancaster / Lancaster Grill	11 Goswell St	1922
Earl of Leicester	30 Infirmary Sq	1901
Elephant & Castle	Thurlaston	1862
Everard Arms	Cottingham Rd, Corby	1956
Exeter Arms	Uppingham	1978
Fairfield	Gloucester Crescent	1966
Falcon	Long Whatton	1953
Fernie Lodge	Husbands Bosworth	1991
Ferrers Arms	Derby	1979
Firs	Wigston	1959
Forest Rock	Woodhouse Eaves	1947
Foresters Arms	17 Frog Island	1895
Forge / Griffin Inn	Glenfield	1888
Fountain	Sileby	1924
Fox & Goose	Illston On The Hill	1978
Fox & Hounds	Exton	1978
Fox Inn	Oadby	1897
Free Trade Inn	Sileby	1923
Freemasons Arms	Braunstone Gate	1889
Gate Hangs Well	Syston	1924
George	Desborough	1882
George & Dragon	Newbold Verdon	1902
Gladstone Arms	Hill St	1901
Glen Inn	Glen Parva	1959
Globe	Silver St	1887
Golden Fleece	Stamford	1978
Golden Fleece	Upper Broughton	—
Golden Lion	26 Highcross St	1919
Green Dragon	Lincoln	1991
Green Man	Stamford	1978
Griffin Inn	Swithland	1947
Griffin Inn	Glenfield	1888
Half Time Orange	Burnmoor St	1997
Haunch of Venison	Leamington Spa	1995
Hearty Goodfellow	Southwell	1992
Heathcote Arms	Croft	1920
Hermitage	Oadby	1965
Honeycomb	Derby	1975
Horse & Panniers	North Luffenham	1978
Horse & Trumpet	Wigston	1929
Horseshoe Inn	Oakham	1978
Hotel Victory	Holy Bones	1925
Hurdler	Stamford	1978
Inn on the Lawn*	Lincoln	1991
Kellys	Leamington Spa	1994
King William	Market Harborough	1895
King William IV	Enderby	1904
King William IV	Earl Shilton	1869
Kings Head Inn	Burley's Lane	1894
Kings Head Inn	Archdeacon Lane	1895
Knights Lodge	Corby	1978
Lancaster Arms	Desford	1923
Leicester Tiger	Wigston	1955

The Waterside Inn, Mountsorrel

The Bradgate, Newtown Linford

The Lancaster Arms, Desford

The Free Trade Inn, Sileby

The Victory, Aylestone Road, Leicester

Pub	Location	Traded From
Lesters / Lively Lady	Ethel Rd	1970
Lindens	Mountsorrel	1954
Loggerheads	16 Lower Redcross St	–
Lord Bassett Arms	Sapcote	1883
Lord Clifden	65 Mill Lane	1888
Malt Shovel	8 Lower Church Gate	1930
Maltings / Gallant Knight / Old Knightthorpe Inn	Loughborough	1973
Manners Arms	Grantham	1992
Marquis of Granby	Welford Rd	1889
Marquis of Granby	Waltham On The Wolds	1969
Marquis Wellington	139 London Rd	1893
Maynard Arms	Bagworth	1902
Mermaid	St Albans	1994
Midland Arms	Fox St	1889
Mill Lane Tavern	1e Mill Lane	1912
Mill on the Soar	Broughton Astley	1988
Millstone Inn	Barnack	1978
Mitre & Keys	Lower Red Cross St	1931
Molly O'Grady's / Saracens Head	Hotel St	1903
Nags Head	Glenfield	1896
Nags Head & Star / Oxford Boater	72 Oxford St	1919
Narborough Hotel	Narborough	1881
Nelson	Humberstone Gate	1889
Neville Arms	Medbourne	1910
New Cattle Market / Cattle Market Hotel	53 Aylestone Rd	1892
New Inn	Enderby	1887
New Plough	2 Lower Churchgate	1930
Old Black Horse Inn	Houghton	1914
Old Castle / Castle Inn	12 Castle View, Newarkes	1935
Old Crown	Fleckney	1920
Old Horse	162 London Rd	1894
Old Mitre	1 Lower Red Cross St	1903
Old Robin Hood	19 Woodgate	1888
Old Star	Sharnford	1919
Old Vic	Nottingham	1996
Old White Swan	Newbold Verdon	1862
Paget Arms	Loughborough	1971
Peacock	Croxton Kerrial	1969
Pelican	Gallowtree Gate	1890
Plough	Bagworth	1911
Plough	Enderby	1885
Plough	Littlethorpe	1886
Plough Inn	Duxford	1992
Quay	Bede Island	1998
Queen Victoria	Syston	1922
Queens Head	Saddington	1970
Queens Head	Billesdon	1978
Racehorse	Warwick	1988
Racehorse	Northampton	1973
Radnor Arms	London	1984
Railway Inn	Ratby	1903
Railway Inn	Broughton Astley	1930
Recruiting Sergeant	Great Gonerby	1992
Red Admiral / Station Hotel	Broughton Astley	1924
Red Cow	Hinckley Rd	1908
Red Lion	Huncote	1916
Red Lion	Sturton By Stow	1992
Reindeer	Stamford	1978
Richard III / King Richard III	Highcross St	1895
Rocket	Stephenson's Drive	1959
Roebuck	Earl Shilton	1893
Roebuck	Desford	1909
Rose & Crown	Lutterworth	1898
Rose & Crown	Humberstone Gate	1903
Rose & Crown	Thurnby	1915
Rose & Crown	Histon	1992
Rose & Crown / Loughborough Hotel	Baxter Gate, Loughborough	1922
Royal Hotel	9 Horsefair St	1923

Pub	Location	Traded From
Royal Lancer	47 Asylum St	1894
Royal Oak	Rothley	1920
Royal Oak	Cossington	1934
Royal Oak	Duddington	1978
Royal Oak / Spanish Blade / Sheriff	Kirby Muxloe	1901
Rutland & Derby Arms	15 Millstone Lane	1921
Rutland Arms	Wharf St	1917
Rutland Arms	Hoby	1930
Sailors Return	120 West Bridge St	1897
Shah of Persia	Cumberland St	1888
Shakespeare	Braunstone	1956
Shakespeare Inn	Repton	1923
Sir Frank Whittle	Lutterworth	1969
Sir Robert Peel	50 Jarrom St	1901
Sir William Peel / Lord Nelson	Sandy	1994
Soar Bridge Inn / Railway	Barrow	1888
Sportsman	Western Park	1978
Stag	Barkston	1992
Stamford Arms	Groby	1921
Star & Garter	Wigston	1890
Sun Inn	Church Gate	1922
Sun Inn	Cottesmore	1978
Sun Inn	Gotham	1971
Swallow	Thurnby	1964
Talbot Inn	Gretton	1978
Tower Vaults	4 Humberstone Gate	–
Thomas Cook	Narborough Rd	1973
Three Crowns	Somerby	1978
Three Horse Shoes	Twyford	1929
Three Nuns / Eagle Inn	Loughborough	1954
Tollemache Arms	Buckminster	1969
Tom Thumb	Blaby	1960
Tram Depot	Cambridge	1991
Tudor	Tudor Rd	1901
Unicorn Inn	Carrington St	1913
Van Damme Bar / Great Central Hotel / Nags Head	Northgate St	1897
Vernon	Nottingham	–
Victory / Bedford Hotel	11 Aylestone Rd	1902
Vikings Tun	Wigston	1972
Waterside / Duke of York	Mountsorrel	1922
Wayfarers	Kettering	1972
Welcome Inn	–	1894
West Bridge Tavern	27 West Bridge St	1899
Westcotes Hotel	48 Latimer St	1892
Western	Western Rd	1895
Wheatsheaf	Edith Weston	1995
Wheatsheaf	Thurcaston	1919
Wheatsheaf Inn	Oakham	1979
White Hart	Billesdon	1887
White Hart	Wharf St	1906
White Horse	Quorn	1922
White Horse	Silverstone	1995
White Lion	Whissendine	1978
White Lion	Colsterworth	1969
White Swan	Whetstone	1889
White Swan	Stoke Golding	1894
White Swan	Mountsorrel	1922
William Caxton	Derby	1976
Willoughby Arms	Little Bytham	1978
Willow	Humberstone Lane	1961
Willow Tree	3 Willow St	1890
Winstanley Arms	Braunstone	1963
Woodmans Arms	Rutland St	–
Ye Olde Bulls Head	Broughton Astley	1950

Pubs highlighted are currently in the Everards estate.

* Current Leasehold

The Mill on the Soar, Broughton Astley

The Dog & Gun, Keyham

The Quay, Bede Island, Leicester

The Green Dragon, Lincoln

The Knights Lodge, Corby

All dates shown are believed to be accurate. Where dates are omitted, relevant documentation has not yet been validated.

The Everards Company Philosophy

Our Philosophy

We are and will remain an independent private company with active family involvement securely underpinned by our ownership and development of freehold properties.

Our Aim

Our aim is to increase the real worth and profitability of the company in the long term by:-

Providing first class quality goods and services to our customers

Providing caring, rewarding and enjoyable employment for all our staff

Making a beneficial contribution to the communities in which we trade.

EVERARDS
— ESTABLISHED 1849 —

WILLIAM *m* Mary Ann Billson

John Billson — Sophia Louisa *m* Arthur Turle — THOMAS WILLIAM *m* Florence Muriel Nickisson

WILLIAM LINDSAY *m* Ione Beresford Armstrong

Bettyne Ione

m (1) Lord Newtown-Butler   *m* (2) Richard Peter Michael Spencer

PATRICK ANTHO[NY] WILLIAM BERESF[ORD]

Georgina Ione   Denyne Gillian Patricia   Serena Anne *m* Anthony Charles Richards   RICHARD ANTHON[Y] SPENCER EVERAR[D]

Edward Anthony   James Charles   Harry Patrick   Charlotte Ione